The Reluctant Buddhist

by

William Woollard

Grosvenor House
Publishing Limited

The book cover picture is copyright to Gopa & Ted2 Los Angeles, Inc.

This book is published by
Grosvenor House Publishing Ltd
28-30 High Street, Guildford, Surrey, GU1 3HY.
www.grosvenorhousepublishing.co.uk

A CIP record for this book
is available from the British Library

ISBN 978-1-906210-35-9

Dedicated to Daisaku Ikeda for his constant inspiration, and to Sarah Woollard for her constant love and support

Preface.

A year or so ago, Bill Gates was reported as saying in one of his public speeches that *"being worth 27 billion dollars is no fun."* It's a great throwaway line of course, and it was no doubt intended as such. And yet…coming from the man at the top of the capitalist heap so to speak, we should not ignore the kernel of truth it conveys. The fact is that the sentiment expressed is very much in keeping with the picture that has emerged from extensive research carried out by some of America's and Europe's leading psychologists and social scientists, over the past half dozen years. It would seem that the rapidly increasing levels of wealth over the past 50 years or so, particularly in the developed areas of the world such as America and Europe and Japan, are not in any way matched by increasing levels of personal happiness. Indeed, if anything the reverse is true; anxiety levels have soared, in part at least because of the unsettling power of trying to keep up with the Jones's. They've even coined a scientific name for this particular brand of unhappiness; it's called 'reference anxiety.'

That paradox might be hard to swallow at first glance, but it has become so firmly authenticated by the wide ranging research, that it has moved out of the scientific journals, into the public arena. There's more to happiness than financial security, write the social scientists, to find themselves now being echoed by the politicians, declaring that there must be more to their policies than simply a concern for GDP!

But it's not just wealth. The fact is that on almost any criterion you might select, we have more these days than ever before, more just about anything, more comfort, more holidays, more leisure, more partners, more food, more houses, more health. But not it seems, more happiness.

So what might we conclude from this? It would seem that the great consumerist, materialist, grab-what–you-can-while-you-can ethos of the 80's and 90's may still have a long way to run, but it's no longer on its own. Today there would seem to be a strong counter-current gathering momentum, with people increasingly saying that there must be more to life than just acquiring more *stuff*; yet another flat-screen TV or another new car in the drive.

That, essentially, is what this book is about. The *something more*.

This is a serious, committed, personal account of Buddhism, but only in the sense that Buddhism is about daily life. Thus it is not in any way about a remote, abstract, inaccessible, impractical philosophy. Essentially it is about some of the most basic and universal of human wishes, such as the fundamental desire for a stronger and more consistent sense of well being at the core of one's life. It's about the crucial importance of a sense of connectedness and of genuine engagement with other people, and a concern for their well being too. About the life transforming power of purpose, and of gratitude, and of hope, and the intimate relationship between a sense of optimism and good health. And much more.

Put simply, *The Reluctant Buddhist* is about *happiness* in this life; about learning, in a wholly practical way, how to build a better and happier life for yourself and others, no matter what the circumstances you find yourself in. You certainly don't have to be especially knowledgeable, or dedicated, or indeed religious in any way.

For Buddhism teaches the extraordinary truth that happiness is not a matter of chance or of accident, but essentially a matter of *choice,* and that we can all learn how to make that choice. Indeed, one of the most remarkable things for me, as I went about the research for this book, was the realisation that many of the findings that have come out of the modern research, into what it is that makes people feel good about themselves, and experience a sense of wholeness and purpose in their lives, are prefigured in the principles and the practice of Buddhism.

Why then the *Reluctant* in the title? Because it took me a long time to realize the value of what I had come into contact with completely by chance. At the time I simply didn't want it, or see any need for it in my life. That is one of the main themes in the book. It is a starting position that, I believe, many casual readers will share with me. There are, I feel sure, lots of reluctant Buddhists about.

Acknowledgements

In the journey from conception to realisation many people have played a part, in so many ways, in the writing of this book. I would like to express my sincere thanks to all my Buddhist friends in London who, in conversations and discussions at meetings over the past few years, have contributed many of the thoughts and the ideas that are expressed here. My gratitude is particularly due to Kazuo Fujii, friend and teacher, for always being there for me, and to Barbara Cahill, who will no doubt be surprised to read this, because she cannot know just how much her brilliant commentaries were the inspiration of my early practice.

But above all my thanks must go to Guy McCloskey and Jason Henninger and their colleagues from SGI-USA who have made a truly immense contribution in reading and commenting on the text in such detail, and to Jessica, my agent, who has been a constant inspiration with the warmth of her encouragement and the accuracy of her advice. Thank you all so much.

A note on the author.

Producer, director, writer, presenter, William Woollard's career covers the entire spectrum of television production, but he has experienced several other careers in an eventful life. Oxford graduate. A fighter pilot with the RAF. A trouble shooter for an oil company in the jungles of Borneo and the deserts of Oman. A social scientist working on corporate social responsibilities with major international organisations in Europe and the USA. Finally, an award-winning television presenter and writer, producing documentary programmes for many of the world's foremost networks in Europe and America.

Much travelled. Twice married. Four children. A life time interest in comparative religion among many other things. He writes," I came to Buddhism with the deepest scepticism about its appropriateness or relevance in a modern western environment. I am wholly convinced of its profound value to any life, anywhere. I see that initial scepticism as perhaps my primary qualification for writing this book."

Contents

CONTENTS

CHAPTER ONE

What do We Mean By Buddhism?

Astonishment is the origin of philosophy, and no doubt of science too; astonishment at the detail of daily life, and at the sheer breadth and scope of the universe within which that life is played out. There is something of that astonishment on first getting to grips with Buddhism. It is full of surprises. It doesn't fit into any of the stereotypes that most of us acquire through travel and casual study. It's not remote. It's not academic. It's not passive. It's not dull. It *is* radical and challenging and active and yes... surprising. It is above all about learning how to make the detail of everyday life richer and more fruitful.

But that is written after many years of Buddhist practice. When I first encountered Buddhism in the UK, I remember all too clearly the strong sense of alienation that it inspired. It just didn't fit. I didn't want it. I didn't need it. I didn't have the time for it. And in any case, I knew profoundly that it wasn't in the slightest way relevant to my hectic life style, however interesting I knew it to be as a body of thought.

I had lived and worked overseas for many years in South East Asia and the Middle East among Buddhists and Hindus and Muslims, and I was aware of the beauty of much Buddhist thought and how well it fitted into the rhythms of the local life in which it had been born and nurtured for centuries.

What I needed more than anything was more space, not more clutter. I knew who I was, and pretty much what I wanted from life, which was essentially more of the same. I wanted more success, more fame, more wealth, so that I could have more unencumbered time. I was pretty much addicted to the excitement and the pace of the career I had ended up in; writing and producing and presenting television programs. Every program was both demanding and stressful and yet immensely stimulating and rewarding. The creative process was very like a drug. The endless demands on my time or my energies simply served to feed the habit. I didn't want the buzz to go away. I seized more work as it came along, even though I was aware that I already had more than enough to fill my plate.

Television also brought with it many other things to keep the addiction bubbling along nicely, a wide network of strong and interesting acquaintances and relationships, and more than my fair share of the worlds material goods.

Was I happy? If I had been asked that question I would probably have deflected it, rather than answer directly. It wasn't a question I was likely to put to myself. I got on with my life. As it happens, I had been extremely unhappy for several years because of the breakdown in my marriage, which I had believed was immensely strong, well founded and a source of great joy to me.

I took the pain full on and I sort of muddled through. I didn't know of any other way of handling it. I took what life presented to me. I worried deeply about the problems and

2

I laughed as loudly as I dared about the joys. Life was very much a roller coaster, and like the real thing, sometimes it scared the living daylights out of you, and at others it filled you with exhilaration. I remember particularly making sure that I didn't actually use the "happiness" word very often. As soon as you had uttered it, it seemed, whatever it was that you were seeking to describe, had passed you by or evaporated into thin air, better not to pin a label on the experience.

Although I had been brought up in an actively Christian household, and my life, I believed, was informed largely by Christian values, I had long since given up on religion as providing any kind of support or source of help when the going got tough. I didn't feel the need for any religious scaffolding to support my life. My choices were essentially material and intellectual ones. We live in an intellectual age and I knew, pretty much as if it were an absolute truth, that the way to deal with problems and crises of whatever sort was to unravel them intellectually, *think* them through step by step until you had worked out a solution of sorts.

I would rarely if ever have admitted to myself, or to anyone else for that matter, that there were many occasions when that solution just didn't arrive. I would often end up chasing a problem round and round inside my head looking for a way out when none appeared. The result might often be a profound weariness of spirit, the heaviness that comes with unrelieved anxiety. Or, on many occasions, a profound frustration, that might suddenly flash out, unleashed like a thunderclap, upon anything within range. When things went wrong in my life, I looked around for someone else or something else to foist the blame onto. At least that provided a channel for the frustration. I was often described as being angry or abrasive in those days, although I chose to interpret that as meaning that I won a lot of arguments, which I didn't take to be a negative quality. On many occasions for example, on location with a film crew, I would often go out of my way to ensure, very early on, that it was clear who was making the decisions. I saw that as the only way of achieving the kind of quality or the results that I was seeking, in the time and with the resources that were available. I knew I wasn't easy to work with, but I had convinced myself that the friction that resulted was a relatively small price to pay, provided I could achieve the results that were needed.

That basically, was the *me* who encountered Buddhism, through the young lady who was my partner at that time. Although I saw it as being hugely irrelevant to the lives we were leading, it didn't go away. Sarah was very strongly attracted to Buddhist teachings, and began to go to meetings of various kinds. The effect on me was very considerable. Basically I moved from rejection to antagonism. Buddhism had somehow become a distinct threat to the somewhat shaky stability that I was struggling to re-establish in my life after the pain and turmoil of the divorce. "Buddhism. Who needs it?" I thought, "I've got enough problems as it is!"

But it wasn't that simple. Exasperation and anger were not enough. The dilemma I faced was that in order to ensure that it was rejected and pushed out of our lives on a wholly rational basis, I had to know much more about it. In short, I had to study Buddhism to be able to argue convincingly its irrelevance and inappropriateness to the nature of our daily life.

This book is really my attempt to chart what has happened since then.

This isn't in any way a step-by-step account. I had no real sense of being on a journey. It is only when I look back that I can see the distance that I have travelled and how deeply the change has penetrated into my life. There wasn't in any way a damascene moment of change, or anything approaching that. It was a relatively slow process, spread over a couple of years of talking and reading, of arguing, oh so much arguing, and rejecting and re-assessing. It wasn't a soft journey. Not at all. The reluctance within me was strong, for all the commonplace reasons. I didn't *need* religion, least of all something as outlandish and ostensibly alien as Buddhism. I didn't want to be part of a defined group that might impinge in the slightest on what I saw as my individuality. Above all I simply didn't believe that what is described as the Buddhist practice could have any enduring effect on the way I lived and felt about life. How could it? How could a practice as, well, as bizarre and as seemingly mindless as repetitive chanting change my life from the inside out?

And yet, as I studied and discussed and argued, there was so much about Buddhism that made sense. The underlying values were quite clearly valuable; they were aimed at creating the sort of compassionate, constructive, value-creating society in which one would choose to live and bring up children. And I could see its effect upon people I began to encounter at meetings and seminars. They clearly sought to be positive and resourceful about their lives, even when they were deeply embroiled in problems.

And they were immensely generous and supportive in their approach to other people. There was none of the abrasiveness and the corrosive cynicism that we encounter so frequently in today's society.

I gradually became aware that I had reached one of those genuine life moments. One of those difficult moments when you realize that you are going to have to make what could well be a life-changing decision, however much you feel that you would rather not be in that position at all.

It is so difficult to achieve profound change in our lives. Indeed it is perhaps *the* most difficult thing. Here I was, with my life seemingly set on a well-defined course, comfortable, moderately successful, with no perception of religious need, and yet I had encountered something that looked as if it could possibly bring immense richness and depth into my life, and the lives of those around me. The awareness of the potential didn't make the inner struggle any easier.

These days I meet many people who are in a very similar position. Many who are looking for something *extra* in their lives, something only vaguely expressed perhaps, and ill-defined, but none the less real and persistent. I meet them all the time. People of all ages, young and old; many of them people who on most counts would seem to have just about everything one could wish for. And yet, when you get closer to them, there is often this edge of malaise. Nothing serious, just a perception of something missing, that might offer a wider and a deeper and more profound dimension than can ever come from the repeated rituals of work and play, or dealing with all the material concerns that swallow up so much of our day.

There is just so much to do these days, and so much available to be done, that it is all too easy to have our lives almost entirely taken up with "stuff;" by the doing and the arranging and the moving swiftly on from one meeting, one event, one party, one pub, to another. But we are undoubtedly spiritual animals. However much we try to persuade ourselves to the contrary. The physical and the material are simply not enough. There's a gap. Even that powerful lady who sang so confidently in the 80s,

"This is a material world
...and I am a material girl"

has sought subsequently, the consolations of a powerful religion.

There was a time perhaps, not all that long ago, when that, or something close to it, would have been the answer for the vast majority of us, when that other dimension would have been provided for us by the religions that underlie all our societies. But that doesn't seem to be the case any more. Certainly not religion in any formalised sense. We still feel the need for the profound spiritual experience, but more and more we reject the structure and the formalism that comes with most religions. Strange as it may seem that dimension is more often to be met these days by the ever-increasing lines of books in the *self-help* section of the local book shop, with their various forms of instant advice on how we might enrich or deepen or give some clearer direction to our lives. How else explain the booming sales of books that purport to tell us how to live?

I trust my Buddhist friends will forgive me when I write that Buddhism, in a sense, has a foot in *both* camps. It is an extraordinary bridge. It has the bed-rock of a profound and all embracing philosophy that touches upon every area of human life. But it is also just as genuinely about self-help.

Indeed, the very heart of Buddhism lies in teaching *oneself* how to handle the business of living more successfully.

I am acutely aware of this in meeting people. Whenever we get to talking casually about Buddhism, there is very often a spark of interest. People want to know more than be conveyed in a brief conversation. And yet at the same time there is often a reluctance to get involved with something as seemingly alien and other-worldly as Buddhism. I can wholly empathise with that view. No one wants to seem weird to his friends. I didn't. For all the claims about our living in a multicultural society, the underlying cultural fabric of Europe is still Western Christianity. Indeed that is true of the entire ex-European empire spread around the globe, from the Americas to Australia. One typical manifestation of that deep cultural inheritance is that somebody who might never go to church from one year to the next, is nonetheless, completely at home, slipping in to a church for a moment of peace, or even, in a moment of stress, offering a prayer to a god he doesn't really know. That same person would find it infinitely more difficult, if not impossible, to slip into any place Buddhist, to chant or to meditate. More importantly, it means that for most of us in the West, when we hear the word Buddhism we don't have any familiar markers to hang onto. With Christianity, even for complete non-Christians, there are plenty. Whereas the mention of the name Buddhism summons up not much more than a series of vague stereotypes; a vast, nebulous, mystical philosophy without any clear boundaries, images of ornate temples in South East Asia, filled with immense, god-like statues of the Buddha, throngs of saffron-robed priests in Thailand, or prayer wheels turning in Tibet.

Hence the question this chapter poses, what do we mean by Buddhism?

Buddhism and Other Religions

You can often get a clearer picture of something, by knowing what it's not, as well as what it is. So, in talking about Buddhism it helps to compare it in part at least, with the religions we may know more about. In doing so I ought to make it clear that in no way am I expressing value judgements, merely observations. I find myself in entire agreement with a statement once made by the late, great, humanist historian and philosopher Arnold Toynbee, when he wrote,

"...the incompatibility between the Buddhist and the Judaic vision of ultimate reality does not indicate that either of these visions is false. It seems to me to indicate only that each vision, being human, is partial and imperfect"

Agreed.

Buddhism is atheistic, or humanistic. That is to say it does not have at its heart the all-seeing, all-powerful creator-god figure that is common to many of the worlds major religions such as Christianity, Judaism, Islam and Hinduism.. The precise form of the divine nature varies of course from one religion to another, but in general terms, the arrangement is that on the one hand there is the God or gods who are responsible for all of creation and who have therefore an immensely powerful role to play in the lives of men. On the other hand there is all of humanity, and the two, gods and humanity...that is to say us, and are separated by an un-bridgeable gulf. It is unthinkable that men can ever become gods. Communication across this gulf from the gods is at least initially in the form of commandments, things that need to be done if one is to lead the good life. Communication from mankind is in the form of prayer, in praise or in supplication. And the basic purpose of life is for people to establish the appropriate relationship with god, both in terms of praise and thanksgiving for the gift of life, and supplication for help when life's problems become overwhelming. The concept of the anthropomorphic Christian God has of course evolved over the centuries, but at the heart of Christian services there is still very much the sense of the divine father figure, who has bestowed life upon all men. The prayer spoken at funerals makes it clear that *"the Lord giveth and the Lord taketh away."*

Buddhist humanism by contrast is rooted in the lives of ordinary people. You will sometimes hear it called *dynamic humanism,* because its primary purpose is to move people's whole lives towards the positive end of the spectrum. But the essential point is that it explicitly denies the existence of a creative force outside human life. All Buddhas therefore are ordinary human beings. They may be extraordinary in terms of their wisdom and the profound depth of their perceptions, and their ability to lead others, but they make no claims to divine powers or connections. They don't claim at any time to have a hot line to God. Indeed they constantly stress their ordinary humanity. Conversely, Buddhism teaches, all ordinary human beings have within them the potential for Buddhahood, potential being a key word. Buddhahood is not about perfection or elevation of any kind. It is described as being simply a powerful quality or a resource we have within us, that we need to learn how to harness or make use of, in our lives. Thus Buddhism is essentially about empowering people, enabling them to use *all* the resources they have, spiritual as well as intellectual, to create value in their own lives and the lives of others. To increase if you like, the sum total of human happiness.

There are of course many profound implications that arise from Buddhism's basic humanism. Since it isn't about God or Gods, for example, we have to be careful about how we use and respond to words like *"faith"* and *"prayer"* that occur so commonly in the writings on all religions, including Buddhism. You will find them everywhere. But if there isn't a god to have faith in, or to pray to, then clearly these words will mean something very different in Buddhism.

Or take the issue of inter-religious conflict, which is undoubtedly one of the greatest and one of the most challenging issues of our age. Since Buddhism is not attached to any particular definition of divinity, it doesn't have any boundaries. Nothing and no one is excluded. It doesn't have the boundaries for example that can separate the Islamic definition of divinity from the Christian, or the Christian from the Judaic, or the Judaic from the Hindu. It is wholly inclusive and in this sense it is a colossal vision. It reaches out to embrace every man's relationship with himself, man and society, society and the environment, the environment and the Universe. You might think of it almost as a set of concentric circles radiating out from the self, the individual, and stretching to the furthest reaches of the Universe.

The second marker, if I may call it that, that had a profound effect upon me was the realisation that this Buddhism is not a morality. That is to say it doesn't have a set of religious dogma or commandments that have been laid down by some external authority, to define how we should go about our lives. That is undeniably a crucial distinction, because we are so accustomed to the idea that religions come with rules of behaviour attached.

Christianity for example has its commandments. Islam and Judaism have strict codes that cover details of everyday living such as what you can eat and when. Hinduism, even in the modern India, has its god-given caste system that would seem to lock people into particular roles in society for life-time after lifetime, as priests and soldiers, rulers and merchants and workers.

At the heart of Buddhism is the profound realisation that there is no black and white separation between good and evil. Everybody has both. There is good and evil, there are positive and negative forces potentially in all things, all the time. The constant struggle that we are involved in is to rec-ognize our negativity for what it is. That recognition is the very first step in moving our lives away from it, towards what is positive and value creating. The Buddhist practice is offered essentially as the *mechanism* to help us towards that, because it is undeniably a tough business. Our inherent negativity is immensely compelling and persuasive, and ever-present.

Thus, Buddhism is not prescriptive. It is by contrast obser-vational, very much in the sense that science is observa-tional, without in any way wishing to push that compari-son too far. Science for example sets out to define pre-existing physical laws of the Universe such as the law of light say, or the law of gravity. Whether or not we know about, or understand, or accept the laws of gravity, if we choose to walk out of a fifth floor window, then undoubt-edly, the law of gravity will have an impact upon our lives.

In a similar way, Buddhism sets out to define what might be called the universal spiritual laws of life; the principles that drive human thought and behaviour. Then essentially it says, It is your life. Only *you* can live it. No one else can do it for you. Only you can resolve all the influences that come to bear on you, during your life's journey. No one else can. And thus only you can be *responsible* for the *way* in which you resolve those influences. And just as the law of gravity is strict in the physical Universe, so, in Buddhism is the principle of personal responsibility.

Central to Buddhism is the idea that we are wholly responsible for the causes that we make, good, bad and indifferent. And wholly responsible for the effects that those causes inevitably plant in our lives, good bad and indifferent. In some place, at some time those effects will make themselves felt. Indeed Buddhism teaches that the causes and effects are attached to us as closely if you like as our shadow is, and just as we can't walk away from it, so it says, we can't walk away from them.

It is undoubtedly one of the toughest Buddhist principles to take on board and to live with. It is both immensely refreshing, in terms of not laying down a code of behaviour, and yet immensely challenging, in terms of assigning personal responsibility. It is also a teaching that is, paradoxically, full of hope. When things go awry in our lives for example, it's very natural for us to cast around for someone or something else to blame for whatever has gone wrong. We all do it. Buddhism however argues that we need to look within ourselves for the causes, because they will be there. The key point being, if the causes are within is, so too are the *remedies.*

The third characteristic that helps I think to define Buddhism for those who have had little contact with it, is that Buddhism is not passive. This runs directly counter to what is perhaps one of the most enduring stereotypes of Buddhism that colours almost any discussion of it. Buddhism *is* pacifist, because it believes strongly that war and violence are wholly destructive and serve only to create and perpetuate more violence and destruction. But "pacifism" is often taken to contain within it so to speak "passivism." Hence the commonly held stereotype that Buddhism is essentially a form of *escapism*, and that Buddhists are likely to be quiet, withdrawn and somewhat diffident people, mainly intent upon seeking some sort of way out, some sort of refuge from the pace and harshness of modern life.

Nothing could be further from the truth Buddhism is a huge and all-inclusive philosophy, so it certainly provides plenty to think about, but above all Buddhism is about *action*, about the way people live their lives rather than simply the way they think them. So it is constantly challenging people out of their comfort zone, to look for new ways of developing and realising their own potential and new ways of creating value in their lives, and the lives of those around them. It is about a self-belief.

So, to sum up briefly, Buddhism is atheist, it does not involve belief in a higher, divine power. It is not a morality, it doesn't lay down a moral code or a set of dogma or commandments to instruct people how to live their lives, and it is not passive. It constantly challenges us to engage fully with our own lives and the workings of society we live in.

I encounter many people who are travelling on their own roller coasters, up and down and around. Getting on with their lives, more or less successfully. They may have little interest in any religious dimension, apart perhaps from the ritual attendances at christenings and marriages and funerals. They may know little or nothing about Buddhism, and they probably have only a slight inclination to know more. What they do know only too well is that life is tough, and full of challenges to the spirit, for every one of us including those

who seem to be the most successful and the most self confident. And often there is another question quietly but persistently tugging away within, *"Is this all there is to life? Shouldn't
there be something more than this?"*

Buddhism would argue that it is indeed about finding that
something else that so many people feel is missing. As one
Buddhist text puts it so neatly:

*"We ordinary people can see neither our own eyelashes which
are so close, nor the heavens in the distance. Likewise, we do not
see that the Buddha exists in our own hearts."**

That, in a nutshell, is what Buddhist practice and study are
about; learning how to gain access to that inner resource,
how to dig if you like, below the level of the intellect, to
release more of the qualities that make up our full humanity.

There is a very interesting oblique observation on this inner
world made by the man I quoted from earlier, the historian
and philosopher Arnold Toynbee, in conversation with
Daisaku Ikeda, who is one of the greatest modern authorities on Buddhism, many of whose books you will find listed
in the bibliography.

Professor Toynbee makes the crucial point that if we wish to
understand the way our minds work, and the motivations
and impulses that lie behind our thoughts and actions,
there is a great deal that we might learn from Asian philoso-
phies that go back to the time of the first historically
recorded Buddha, Shakyamuni,

"Consciousness" he says, *"is merely the manifest surface of the
psyche. It is like the visible tip of an iceberg, the bulk of which is*

submerged...the discovery and exploration of the subconscious depths of the psyche, which, in the West, started only as recently as Freud's generation, was anticipated in India at least as early as the generation of the Buddha and his Hindu contemporaries, that is to say, at least 2,400 years earlier than Freud....Westerners have much to learn in this field from Indian and East Asian experience."

It has been said that perhaps Buddhism's greatest gift to mankind's spiritual or religious heritage is that it introduced the concept of choice. When Buddhism came into being, some 2500 years ago, that was truly a revolution. At a time when mankind was hemmed in by powerful, controlling, and limiting concepts such as destiny, or the commandments of divine beings, Buddhism introduced this extraordinary idea that we are truly answerable only to ourselves. We have the freedom, and the resource to make our own choices, to take control of our lives provided only that we accept full responsibility for the choices that we make. It was revolutionary then. In many ways, it remains revolutionary today, particularly at a time of fierce religious fundamentalism. It may seem esoteric, outlandish even, to look to Buddhism for a solution to many of society's most intractable problems, but that is largely because our view of Buddhism in the West is limited by so many stereotypes. We have become   accustomed to seeking our solutions not so much in individual change, but through political manoeuvring, or through the promises of science and technology. In essence, Buddhism is about transforming society in the only way that profound change in society can be sustained, from the bottom up, by transforming individual lives. It talks indeed of *human revolution*, individual by individual. One could argue I think, that rarely before in human history, has there been a greater need for a philosophy of life based upon individual responsibility.

The Charter of UNESCO contains a sentiment that echoes the very heartbeat of the Buddhist vision of a world firmly in the grip of peace. The Charter reads,

"...since wars begin in the minds of men, it is in the minds of men that the defences of peace must be constructed."

Buddhism might add the words, *"individual by individual".*

Buddhism and Science.

It has become somewhat fashionable to stitch together the words, Buddhism and science, as if to imply that they occupied to some extent the same or similar territories. I believe that approach to be extremely misleading. Buddhism doesn't claim to be in the least scientific in its approach, nor is it. But then, it doesn't need to be. Buddhism doesn't need scientific justification for its philosophical insights into the nature of human life. And science simply isn't equipped to deal with the area of religious belief. Scientists as individuals may well have religious beliefs, as many of them do of course, but that simply underlines the power of religious thought. Science basically doesn't do religion. It doesn't have the tools to cope with it. The late Stephen Jay Gould, the outstanding American palaeontologist and writer on science actually coined the definitive acronym to describe this position. The acronym is NOMA. It stands for *"non-overlapping magisteria,"* which is a somewhat high-flown way of saying that science and religion essentially occupy different dimensions of our life.

This is I think, an important point, particularly since we live in a world that seems to be totally dominated by science and technology. But the plain fact is that academic science is only a very small and highly specialised part of what we all know. Most of our knowledge comes from our experience of life, and if you think about it even briefly, that is the only way that we could get on with and manage our daily lives. As a result of our personal life experiences, we make a constant series of assumptions about ourselves and other people and the world about us, and we constantly update those assumptions, as our experiences accumulate. We learn about life, you might say, from life. The testing of assumptions, or hypotheses in *science* is a specialised outgrowth from that basic approach to life. When it comes to the biggest and most puzzling questions of all, such as, why are we here? Or, is there a purpose and a meaning to life? Or what happens to us after death? We don't turn to science do we? We turn to a completely different area of our lives, which we have labelled as religion.

As an interesting sidelight on this issue, there was a science symposium held in November 2006, at the Salk Institute in La Jolla, California. Attended by many eminent scientists from around the world, it was entitled *"Beyond belief: Science, religion, reason and survival,"* and it considered among a host of other issues the extraordinary question, *"Should science do away with religion?"* What is noteworthy is that by no means all the eminent scientists there spoke in *favour* of the motion. Steven Weinberg, for example, noted cosmologist and Nobel Laureate from the University of Texas at Austin, was one of those who saw some continuing role for religion in our life. He said,

"I'm not one of those who would rhapsodically say all we need to do is to understand the world, look at pictures of the Eagle nebula and it'll fill us with such joy we won't need religion. We will miss religion."

Indeed we would.

But to return to that initial question, the relationship between Buddhism and science, what I find utterly fascinating is the fact that there is an extraordinary number of ways in which Buddhist perceptions, which have come essentially through many centuries of meditation and reflection, seem to prefigure to some extent many modern scientific conclusions that have come from 200 years of rigorous observation and experiment. Buddhism, for example, like science, is full of surprises. They both reveal just how much we can be misled by our conventional common sense and our everyday perceptions.

The fundamental story of modern science is the story of the unexpected; things are rarely, if ever, what they seem. What we experience with our senses, what we *know* to be the hard and fast nature of reality turns out very often not to be the case. That is unquestionably very hard for us to take on board, but it is true. As the theoretical physicist Brian Greene has expressed it, in *The Fabric of the Cosmos*

*"The overarching lesson that has emerged from scientific inquiry over the last century is that human experience is often a misleading guide to the true nature of reality. Lying just beneath the surface of the every day, is a world we'd hardly recognize."**

One could say that this split between perception and reality started way back with Copernicus. He had the devil's own job convincing his peers that the evidence of their own eyes was just plain wrong. The Sun *didn't* revolve around the Earth every day. They couldn't imagine in their wildest dreams a set up where the Earth was doing the revolving. It took his painstaking mathematical observations to prove that what they saw, what we see every day, is just an illusion. Nowadays of course we no longer need convincing of that fact. We simply ignore what our eyes tell us and put our faith in what the scientists tell us. None of us has actually *seen* the Earth revolving round the Sun.

The process has gone on continuously since then. As scientists over the years have peeled away layer after layer of our ignorance to reveal more and more of the way the world really works, so they have revealed a reality that is not just mildly different from our everyday perception, but one that runs directly counter to what we know to be plain common sense. We now know that our hearing for example can detect only a small fraction of the entire spectrum of sounds that is created in the world around us. Our eyes are the same, they can only see a small part of the entire spectrum of electromagnetic waves and can therefore pick up only a fraction of what there is around us to be seen. The world of objects, including ourselves, that we take to be fixed and solid, turns out to be mainly empty space and vibration. And when we venture into the world of the basic particles that make up everything that exists, the real world becomes even more bizarre, even more unstable. Nothing is fixed. Nothing remains the same from moment to moment. Everything is in a constant state of change, particles appearing and disappearing seemingly at random, sometimes being there, sometimes not, sometimes as a particle, sometimes as a wave of energy. Unexpected, unreal even. Einstein at one time considered it to be absurd, but it proves nonetheless to be true. It says a great deal that one of the most important laws that has been defined by scientists themselves, to describe this world that underlies all our realities is called "the uncertainty principle," because this *real* world seems to shift under the scientist's gaze. It changes depending on how and when it is observed.

What has all that got to do with Buddhism? Well quite a bit, I think. As I became more familiar with the world of Buddhist thought it seemed to me that there are some remarkable similarities between that physical, technical, scientific view of the way the world works and many fundamental long-established Buddhist principles. Buddhism also talks of change being the constant rhythm of all things under the Sun, indeed including the Sun. The word it uses is "impermanence." It talks of the separation and yet the unity in the relationship between mind and body and between our self and our environment; two but not- two, it says in an instantly memorable phrase. We can't actually see it, we have to take it on trust. Indeed Brian Greene's phrase about physics is just as apt, applied to Buddhist thinking.

"....experience is often a misleading guide to the true nature of reality."

Thus much of Buddhist teaching is really about getting us to look *again* at some of the ordinary everyday, seemingly common-sense assumptions that we carry around with us, brushing away the film of familiarity, sharpening up the lens through which we see the world, so that we get to see it with a greater degree of clarity. It remains the same old world. It's just that our perception of it is somewhat different, and the changed perception changes fundamentally the way we behave towards ourselves and towards others.

Buddhism and Health

As I mentioned earlier, on the whole, science doesn't do religion. But it is worth adding that over the past few years a growing number of scientists has been showing an interest in religion essentially as an *evolutionary* phenomenon. They are basically asking the question, "Why does religion exist?

What's it all about?"In scientific terms, it is better expressed perhaps as what possible *evolutionary* purpose might it serve. In a sense, it is *the* ultimate question that we have to ask, isn't it? What *is* the primary role of religion in our lives? Why is it there? It is certainly a question that has tugged at my mind continuously throughout my reconciliation to Buddhism, and it runs like a thread through this account.

Karl Marx of course famously derided religion "as the opiate of the masses." That is an undeniably powerful phrase and it has rumbled powerfully down the past few decades, but those few decades are a mere snap of the fingers, compared to the long march of millennia, during which religion in one form or another, lets call it spiritual belief, has clearly played a central role in human life. It would seem to go back indeed to the very earliest roots of our existence, long, long before the first establishment of settlements, and agriculture, and the beginnings of what we like to call recorded civilisation. It is now widely held for example that the extraordinarily rich and emotive cave paintings that are associated with the earliest appearance in Europe of modern man, that is us, some 30 to 40,000 years ago, weren't just there as a kind of decoration, the idle doodling perhaps of some Neolithic hunters with time to spare during a long cold winter. They were, it now seems clear, linked to some kind of ceremony, some profoundly spiritual experience shared by members of a tribe or an extended family, deep in the womb of some cave, with the light of torches flickering off the coloured images on the walls, to bind them more strongly together. Nothing could have been more important to enable a tribal group to cope with the physical and the spiritual challenges of stone age life. However sharp their weapons or their stone tools, they would be as nothing compared to the value of trust and support and belief in themselves, shared between the members of a small and lonely band.

Fast forward 30,000 years or so, to today, and it would seem that one of the most striking benefits to come from strong religious or spiritual belief is that it delivers a greater sense of wholeness and of well being. There seems to be a growing body of evidence to suggest that it makes you feel better and even live longer. Strengthening the immune system, making you less prone to life-shortening illnesses such as cancers and heart disease, better able to cope with life's stresses and strains, and with a faster rate of recovery from stressful events such as medical interventions and serious illness. That is obviously a huge claim, and not one that can be made lightly. It is a question that I return to in more detail later on in the chapter on Buddhism and health, but it is based firmly on a very considerable and growing body of research. As one scientific journal has summarised it;

"Recent sociological studies have shown that, compared with non-religious people, the actively religious are happier, live longer, suffer fewer physical and mental illnesses, and recover faster from medical interventions such as surgery."*

I'm not sure whether or not we might be allowed to apply the term "evolutionary" to this sort of scientific observation, but I don't think anyone would question the fact that it is advantageous. A religious dimension in our life it seems clear, breeds hope, and hope in turn nurtures the body's ability to fight off illness.

The whole of Buddhist practice is aimed at nurturing hope and optimism in our lives.

Buddhism and Daily Life

This is the acid test isn't it? How does Buddhism affect the way we see and the way we deal with the constant stream of events that makes up the daily-ness of our lives, in all its chaotic, unexpected, challenging, sometimes uplifting, often frustrating detail? The answer can be expressed in many ways but one that is clearly uppermost is that Buddhism is both inspirational and practical. It delivers, a view of human life that is overarching and visionary, so that you are in a position to see things from a wider perspective. At the same time it is immensely down to earth, and provides you with a practical, down-to-earth strategy for dealing with daily events.

It *does* make a profound difference when you are aware that Buddhism is not about demonstrating allegiance to some external god-given set of rules and commandments. It is really about allegiance to ones better self. That clearly has the most profound impact on how we relate to ourselves, our sense of self worth if you like, and how we relate to all those around us, family and friends and colleagues.

It *does* make a profound difference that the Buddhist view of the world is all-inclusive. It is genuinely a global religion. It seeks to break down all the barriers between 'self' and 'other.' In that sense it transcends race and ethnic groups and nationalities and cultures, it embraces all of humanity without exception. One could argue that never have we been in greater need of such an all-embracing view of life, of a way to break down barriers between people.

As to being utterly practical and down to earth, it is not in any way about hoping to achieve some place in a heavenly hereafter. Buddhism is *daily life*, so it deals with the here and now. It seeks to engender wholly down-to-earth qualities such as perseverance in the face of setbacks, courage to face up to problems rather than sweeping them under the carpet, and increasing awareness of the value of our neighbour. And it is about balance. We are so accustomed in the West, to separate Caesar and God, State and Church, to believe that spiritual aspirations are separate from, often more worthy than, material ones. Buddhism argues that both are essential to human happiness. One is not more worthy than the other. It is up to us to establish the appropriate balance in our lives.

The implications of those principles, those basic values, are clearly profound, not just for the individual, but for the whole of society. The Buddhist view of reality is that everything but everything in existence is interconnected and interdependent at the most profound level. Everything is fundamentally part of the whole. Just as, on the surface of things, the island seems to be completely separate from the mainland, but go deeper, to the sea bed, and it is seen to be part of the whole. Each wave on the surface of the sea may seem separate and distinct, but each one is embedded in the vast body of the ocean.

As it happens, that deeply rooted Buddhist view, which goes back over 2500 years, also chimes in many ways, with what we are told by modern science. Our DNA for example, connects us to every other living thing, not just to other humans, but to *every* living entity that has ever existed on the face of the planet. As one noted American philosopher scientist, Daniel Dennet, has put it so passionately;

"A virus is a single huge molecule, a macromolecule composed of hundreds of thousands or even millions of parts depending on how small the parts are that we count. These atomic level parts interact

*in their obviously mindless way to produce quite striking effects.
Chief among these from the point of view of our investigation is
self replication. ….There is no longer any serious informed doubt
about this: we are the direct descendants of these self replicating
robots. ….There is just one family tree, on which all living things
that have ever lived on this planet can be found-not just animals
but plants and algae and bacteria as well. You share a common
ancestor with every chimpanzee, every worm, every blade of grass,
every redwood tree."**

That's just for starters, that's just the DNA. The materials of
which we are made connect us intimately to every rock,
every planet, every galaxy in the universe. We are made of
the same stuff. We are, that is to say, truly interconnected
right down to the level of the atom and the molecule. And
this is not just a piece of sophistry, it is nothing more than
a view of reality that goes beyond our personal experience.
We are intimately part of our environment in every way.

But what real difference does it make? What's wrong, you
might well ask, with seeing ourselves as quite separate and
distinct from everything else on the planet? What possible
difference can it make? Science, in proving the reality of our
interconnectedness doesn't of course have an ethical or a
social dimension. Buddhism does, and the fundamental
Buddhist answer to that question would be that everything
in our lives is driven by our perceptions. Thus a gross misper-
ception that arises really from the narrowness of our view,
will lead to grossly inappropriate action.

Close to it simply means *"me"* and *"you."* That's probably
easy enough to handle. Further afield it begins to mean *"us"*
and *"them." "They"* are different from *"us,"* and it begins to
get more difficult. You may well be a mild mannered, chari-

table and altruistic individual who gets on with everybody, but it goes without saying that not everybody is.

It doesn't take more than a brief look at human history, old and new, to see that the idea of separation, of them and us, of their lot and our lot, of white skins and brown skins, of Catholics and Protestants, of Christians and Muslims, lies at the root of everything from the brawling between different tribal groups of football fans outside the pub on a Saturday night, to the powerfully disruptive forces of racism and extreme nationalism and religious fundamentalism. And unspeakable events like Rwanda. And Sebrenica. And Auschwitz.

Buddhism, in effect, draws three concentric circles around our lives. Ourselves, at the centre. Then other people, society as a whole, a global society. Then finally the outer ring of the universal environment. Buddhism argues that they are all intimately interconnected. No one of them is complete without the others. To live a full and happy life we have to be connected to all three. That is to say we have to fully respect our own life, we need to support the lives of others in every way that we can conceive, and we need to protect and preserve the physical environment that sustains us all.

Buddhism and the Dilemma of Suffering

Suffering *is* the human dilemma. We just don't understand it, and we don't know how to cope with it. No one wants suffering. No one wants difficulties and problems in their life. The common sense view therefore is that what we have to do is to eliminate them, insulate ourselves from them, arrange our lives in such a way that they don't trouble us any more.

Once again however, Buddhism presents us with an unusual paradox. Basically it teaches that the problems and the difficulties and the anxiety-making challenges that we all encounter as we go through life, and that we all spend so much time and energy and ingenuity in trying to avoid, are in fact valuable. More than that, they're *essential* to our genuine well being and our true happiness in life. They provide, it argues the *only* available means for getting the very most out of who we are; for becoming the strongest, the happiest, the most resilient and optimistic individual that we are capable of being. If that strikes you as being a somewhat eccentric, not to say perverse proposition, I can only say that that is precisely how it struck me when I first encountered it. Who needs problems?

But of course, *needing* them isn't the issue. Its *handling* them when they occur that gives us so much trouble. When everything is going well it goes without saying that we all prefer to focus on the sunshine and the happiness in our lives. But as we all know only too well, sunshine and happiness are scarcely permanent conditions; reality has a nasty habit of intruding. Love turns to heartbreak, wealth to poverty, harmony to conflict, health to sickness, and peace to war. The plain fact is that we are conditioned in all sorts of ways, pretty much from our earliest childhood, to respond to problems and difficulties negatively, to see them as the bane of our lives, to be avoided almost whatever the cost. But since they inevitably continue to occur in our lives, thick and fast, so does the negative response. It's not unlike Pavlov's dogs. The natural result is that problems and challenges become inextricably associated in our minds with anxiety and concern.

The key to unlocking this situation, Buddhism teaches, is to see the situation for what it really is. It is not so much the problem that is causing the suffering, as the *response* to it. That may seem an unreal distinction but in fact it is a fundamentally important one. So fundamental that once we grasp it, it can change our whole lives from the inside out. Buddhism argues that whether the problem is a cause of suffering or a source of personal growth depends essentially on our *attitude* towards it.

There are of course, plenty of physical parallels. No weightlifter for example, develops greater muscle power by lifting lighter and lighter weights. No athlete can achieve peak fitness by avoiding the pain that comes from the toughest training. Indeed it's commonplace for athletes to talk of pushing themselves through the *pain* barrier. If the athlete chooses to adopt softer and easier routines then he can kiss goodbye to success in competition. To achieve their best performance we take it for granted that athletes and sportsmen have to put themselves through the mill; create the conditions that provide the strongest resistance, or the greatest difficulty, and then push themselves through that resistance, and overcome that difficulty. They emerge *on the other side* as stronger, more resilient, more capable athletes, not to mention happier ones! It doesn't come easily. They have to learn how to do it. That is what training is all about. It's tough.

Buddhism was created out of the perception that life itself is tough, and that how we choose to respond to that toughness determines the nature of our life. Not just for some of us, but for all of us. Without exception. For those who have a generous supply of the world's goods, as well as for those who don't. It's just that the nature of the toughness is different. There is no perfect insulation that we can erect to keep at bay the stresses and strains that come with our humanity. Not status, nor wealth, nor success nor power. Material prosperity may change the superficial circumstances, it may get rid of hunger and cold, but it doesn't change fundamentally the nature of the human condition. We are all, in that sense, in the same boat. And never perhaps has that been more evident than in this so-called age of celebrity, when the lives of those who have the slightest claim to fame are laid bare before us every day of the week in newspapers and on television. Scratch a princess or a prime minister or a movie star, and however glamorous or shining their lives may seem from the outside, the reality is of course that they go through exactly the same pains as the rest of us, indeed more, or more extreme in many cases. Wealth and success bring their own pressures.

The strange thing is that despite all the lessons we get from our own lives, in a never-ending stream, we often choose to deny the reality. We like to see the constant stream of problems and challenges that we face, as being somehow a deviation from the norm.

"This is not really how my life is," we say to ourselves, *"I just have to get through this rough patch, and then things will straighten out. Ill get back onto an even keel."*

We know for certain that once we get over this little local difficulty we happen to be having at the moment; this particular financial crisis or the conflict were having at work, or the argument were involved in with our partner, or whatever, then, we're sure, our life will return to its *normal* state of calm and equanimity. That's the life state we want, a life without problems.

It doesn't exist, of course. The current crop of problems will be replaced by the next crop, and so on. They are as natural a part of our life on this planet, as gravity, and just as apples always fall downwards, so human life is filled with complexity and challenge.

Thus, Buddhism isn't in any way about escapism, about finding some refuge from the thrust and pace and troubling complexity of modern life in some inner meditative sanctuary. Nor is it about stoicism, learning how to tough it out. Or about learning how to remain immensely calm when all around you are losing theirs. None of that, or indeed anything like that. Above all perhaps it is about challenge.

Right at the very heart of Buddhism lies the notion that although we cannot change the inherently challenging nature of human life, it is possible to change fundamentally our *attitude* towards those challenges. That may seem a pretty obvious statement, banal even. "Is that all?" you might ask.

But the difference in attitude, Buddhism argues, is crucial to achieving a difference in *outcome.* Whether a problem that arises in our lives causes suffering, or is seen to be a source of growth depends fundamentally on our attitude, to ourselves first of all, and to the situation that we happen to be in. But as we all know, few things are more difficult to achieve than profound changes in patterns of thought and behaviour that we have spent years grooving into our daily lives. They represent nothing less than who we are, and changing who we are is a tough challenge.

Buddhist practice is focussed essentially on achieving that attitude change. Releasing a whole new source of energy and determination. We can't simply think our way into it. *"From now on I'm going to live like this."* It simply doesn't work. We have to learn how to make the change. Just as the athlete has to train, to grow new muscle and to improve his reflexes, to get the best out of his body, so we have to learn a new set of skills and ways of thinking. It isn't a destination, it's a journey, a continuous journey of self discovery. It starts by accepting responsibility for the bits of our life that are not working, and then developing on a step-by-step, day-by-day basis, resilience courage, and compassion, so that we can face up to the challenge of changing them.

This account is not in any way a series of explanatory lectures on Buddhist philosophy. It is very much an extended conversation; a personal, practical, utterly down-to-earth conversation that follows very much the journey of practice and study that I have taken over the past eighteen years or so, to the point where this practice brings immense value into every area of my life, on a daily basis. It enriches and strengthens my marriage for example, in ways that are too numerous to mention. No marriage is without tension and conflict, in that sense Buddhism is a great marital aid! Or a great partnership aid perhaps, whichever is appropriate. Why? Because arguments between people who share intimately in each others lives can be the most savage and the most fiercely destructive. Both parties know so well the other's vulnerabilities. Buddhist practice delivers into the hands of both parties the most powerful mechanism for bringing those rows to a halt rapidly and healing the wounds. I speak only from experience!

But you don't have to get married to feel the benefits. The same mechanisms, the same approach applies just as powerfully in any environment where people are working together. It has brought a depth and a vitality to my relationships with my children and my friends that I could only have hoped for. It has transformed the way I relate to everybody I encounter in the course of the day, from the newsagent's assistant to colleagues at work.

It hasn't taken away any of the problems or the challenges that are inherent in all our lives. There is nothing seamless about a Buddhist approach to life. Anger, irritation, frustration, disappointment, grief, they all continue as part of the daily mix of emotions. But I see them more clearly for what they are. They don't take over, and there is not the slightest doubt that Buddhism has increased by a vast amount the sum total of happiness in my daily life, and those whom my life touches. Happiness is in many ways a slippery sort of word, because it is so subjective. What indeed is true happiness? But achieving a deeper understanding of what we mean by happiness, the difference for example between what might be called short term rapture over some exciting event, and a sustained, deep- down sense of well being even in the presence of considerable problems, is undeniably important to the way we live our lives. In many ways it is the thread that runs continually through all that follows.

CHAPTER TWO

A Personal Journey

I grew up in an actively Christian household. There had always been a strong religious thread in my upbringing. I didn't go to many church services myself, outside school assemblies perhaps, but there's no question that when I wrote down Christian on my passport application it meant rather more to me than just the fact that I had been baptised in a church. My father's deeply embedded Christian values in particular have had a deep and enduring impact on my life. Not that he ever preached at us. Far from it. He was far too diffident. We all absorbed his values by a kind of osmosis. If I try to think of a single word to capture him, it would be that he was very straight. He had a very clear sense of self; people always knew where they were with him.

Both my parents came from farming stock. They grew up in small close-by villages in the wheat lands of East Anglia, and their early lives were strongly marked by the ebb and flow of the seasons and the closeness and the inter-dependency of village life. People frequently turned to their neighbours for support. That sense of mutual dependence never left them, even when they moved in to London for work, and for better schools for their children. They lived a hard life, with not a trace of ease or luxury, but they never for a moment lost their good humour or their generosity. However difficult their own lives, and it was a constant struggle against poverty, they always had time for others when they sought their help. People, even complete strangers, recognized in my father for example, an unflagging generosity of spirit.

If I look back I can only recall a handful of occasions when we actually discussed his religious beliefs or his principles, but he was always very clear about how carefully we should treat other people. His regular Christian practice has been carried on by my brothers and sisters. For myself, his principles of charity and concern for others have remained an active part of my life, even if they weren't nurtured by regular church going.

My first serious contact with Buddhism occurred many years ago when I was working and living in the Far East. I've always had a keen interest in other religions, on a sort of cultural and archaeological level, and I have spent a substantial part of my working life overseas, in countries which happened to have complex and fascinating religious traditions. I've worked in Israel and Lebanon for example, and Oman and Saudi Arabia in the Middle East, and further afield in Singapore and Hong Kong, China, Indonesia and Malaysia. During those years when I was working closely with teams of people made up of Muslims and Hindus and Buddhists, it was very important to me to find out more about the basis of their religious beliefs.

Then as now in these countries, religious issues were never far below the surface, and very often they boiled over into the streets. Conversations in the canteen, or over the supper table often had a religious or a political edge. So I spent a fair bit of time reading and talking about Islam, and Hinduism and Buddhism, at least until I felt I had more than a superficial understanding of what was going on around me. I worked hard at my conversational Malay and Arabic, and although they were pretty rough, I could, to an extent, hold up my end of the conversation. That made a huge difference to the quality of the human relationships, but my relationship with their religions remained very much an external, intellectual exercise. If I look back I can see that it was prompted by a desire to understand, and to relate to other people at a deeper level than purely work issues, rather than any inner personal interest. I could see just how profoundly these beliefs drove my colleagues lives, but there it ended. I never for a moment considered them as having any relevance to my inner life, or likely to be appropriate to the western life that I related to across the other side of the world. It was the equivalent if you like of having a well-thumbed volume on comparative religion on my bookshelves. It was fascinating to dip into, and I knew pretty well which page to turn to, for this or that bit of information, but once the volume was slotted back into its place, it had no further impact on my life. Whereas my Christianity was somewhat like a well worn jacket; a bit crumpled and loose fitting, and a little thin perhaps at the elbows, but it slipped on easily and once on, it was so habitual I scarcely knew it was there.

However I must say that of the three religions I spent time studying, Buddhism stood out, particularly because of its essential humanism. The Buddha is not divine, despite the innumerable huge golden, god-like statues of the Buddha and Bodhisattvas that adorn the temples of South East Asia. But in its Southern form Buddhism is so hedged about with codes of conduct that the thousands of monks you see in their saffron robes are just about the only people who can possibly devote the time to observing them. Buddhism, it seemed to me at the time, *was* essentially about escaping from the constant challenge and rough and tumble of daily life, into some remote, inner sanctum. Buddhist texts for example talked of meditation as being akin to putting a protective glass sheath around a flickering candle flame, the flickering candle flame being the spiritual awareness of the meditator. Only when it was thus sheltered, presumably from the buffeting winds of reality, could the candle flame begin to burn more brightly. Undoubtedly a beautiful image, but it only served to underline what seemed to me to be the remote and other-worldly quality of Buddhist practice. And when I read Buddhist texts or commentaries, they were obscure and academic in the extreme. What I learned certainly didn't seem relevant to me, to my daily life, my current ambitions, or any future that I envisaged for myself.

It is worth adding here perhaps that the view that I acquired of Buddhism during my five years or so in South East Asia, comes pretty close to the way in which the West has related to Buddhism over the past several hundred years. In general it is true to say that it was this Southern, or Theravada Buddhism, that has tended to colour the general western view of Buddhism ever since. It has been seen, historically speaking, as an extraordinary body of humanist philosophy, full of revealing insights into the forces that drive human behaviour, but remote, academic and obscure in the extreme. In that sense it has been very much more a focus of academic and doctrinal studies than as a guide for daily life, particularly daily life in the cut and thrust of a highly competitive, achievement-driven, post-industrial western society. The prevailing image is of monks turning prayer wheels in some remote mountain top monastery, concerned essentially with escaping from the material dimension of life into some higher reality, through various forms of mental discipline, rather than dealing with the stuff of daily living.

That is of course a stereotype, and undoubtedly inaccurate, but however partial and inaccurate, it was the view that had I developed from my personal experience, even though I was very much a sympathetic observer. Something approximating to it remains, in my experience, the prevailing stereotype held by many people in the West.

There are many forms of Buddhism, just as there are many forms of Christianity, indeed that must rank as one of the main reasons for the somewhat confused image that Buddhism presents in the West. The different schools have different doctrines and codes of practice, but it helps I think, to understand that all forms of Buddhism arise from the same original stem, the teachings of Shakyamuni Buddha, whose story we come to in the next chapter.

Fast forward several years and I encountered Buddhism once again under a completely different set of circumstances. I had been living and working in the UK for many years by now. My marriage of seventeen years had come to a sudden and painful end, so painful in fact that it threatened my stability. The marriage had seemed to me to be nothing short of golden. I was very much in love with my wife, and thought that she was with me. We had three wonderful children, and I thought that we were immensely happy. But I must have been blind. One Friday evening that is still written in stark detail in my memory, I was told that she was seeking a divorce, to go and live with another man, taking our children with her.

I descended into a kind of hell, and to this day, when I think about it, it still has the power to unsettle me.

I have no clear recollection of the sequence of events during the following nine months, other than the fact that I was deeply fearful. I was frightened above all of losing my children and I stumbled blindly through a sort of nervous breakdown. I found it virtually impossible to work, so my job as a television producer and presenter was very much under threat. I could still write the words well enough, but I couldn't deliver them with any conviction to camera any more. When you look into that lens you see a diminutive image of yourself looking back at you, and I found I couldn't look myself in the eye any more, my confidence and my sense of self worth were so badly damaged.

My casual Christianity, I have to say, repaid me for the casualness with which I had regarded it for so many years. It was utterly useless to me in my misery and I was too proud or too scared to seek any sort of professional help. So I just scrambled my way forward, one day at a time, one step at a time, across what seemed to me then to be a sort of grey desert. I wasn't interested in anything that resembled a normal social life or indeed anything very much. My one concern was not to lose my children. Divorced husbands don't fare very well in the custody stakes, particularly when the children are young, as ours were, and expensive barristers are skilled at painting the bleakest of scenarios. But with the children's determination to keep both parent's in their lives, and with their extraordinary understanding of what was really going on, despite their youth, we settled eventually on joint custody. I have a clear memory of standing up in court and berating a judge for seeming to treat so offhandedly, what was to me at that time virtually a matter of life and death, namely the allocation of my children…our children, to one parent or the other. That may sound overly dramatic, but when one is in hell state, life does take on that dramatic black and white quality.

Perhaps I should add right here, before I go on, that one of the greatest benefits of my Buddhist practice is that it has brought an altogether greater clarity of vision. It is very difficult indeed for us to accept our personal responsibility for the circumstances we find ourselves in. At the time I saw this situation very much from the point of view of the victim. This was something that my wife had chosen, for whatever reason, and without any trace of a warning, to inflict upon me. Which made the hell all the more painful. Now, it seems clear, there could only have been such a violent and destructive rupture because both parties had contributed to it in some measure, albeit unwittingly.

A year or so later I had achieved a sort of stability again. I was still depressed and desperately lacking in self-confidence, but I was functioning. I was concentrating on trying to provide a whole life to my children. I learned how to cook a few dishes for example, so that I could cook supper for my children in the evening. Strange as it may seem, this sort of small, utterly inconsequential action really lifted my personal confidence. The fact is that it was positive. I was doing something. Who needed a television career if they could bring up three young kids properly! Nowadays, my children can, and frequently do, laugh hysterically at just how awful those meals were, but at the time, they undoubtedly had a clearer sense of the role that was being played out than I realized. They wiped their plates clean, and filled the kitchen with praise, solely for my benefit. And it worked. I felt useful.

Some of those meals happened to include a lady called Sarah, who can also remember with great clarity, just how awful they were, but she also managed to dig deep and find praise. I wasn't in any way looking for a relationship, but Sarah was young and volatile, and fiercely argumentative, determined it seemed, to drive me out of my despair by sheer energy, even if the relationship didn't survive the therapy. We argued and fought our way from week to week. And many of those arguments, strange as it may seem, were about Buddhism.

Sarah was beginning to take her Buddhist practice ever more seriously. At the time this was no more than a tiny cloud on the horizon of my life. So small in fact that it scarcely registered. All that had occurred was that a close friend of Sarah's who had been practising for some time, had invited her to a couple of meetings, along with his partner. From my position, very much on the margins, the bare bones of the practice seemed to be harmless enough; going to discussion meetings with small groups of people once or twice a month, and the daily practice of chanting an incomprehensible phrase for several minutes at least twice a day, morning and evening. It seemed inconceivable to me that going through this process could achieve what Sarah claimed she was seeking, namely a stronger sense of direction and purpose in her life, and an ability to handle challenges and problems that inevitably came her way, with a greater sense of stability and self confidence.

My appearance in her life must have been one of those challenges. I had found the resources from somewhere to fight my way back into a television career, and I was once again in demand. But I had a great deal of anger about most things, which I rarely chose to suppress. I was prepared to take on anyone who had the nerve to cross me. I suppose I was trying to kid myself that the self-confidence had come back. It hadn't. Every day in front of camera or in front of an audience was a struggle against inner daemons, telling me that I couldn't hack it. Many BBC film crews I'm sure, will remember those days working with me as a kind of hell. "For gods sake lets get it finished before he blows up again," was a   sentiment I overheard on more than one occasion. Above all else I remember being focused on providing a whole life for my children, as if I could, single-handedly, create a shield against all the troubles that had come upon our family.

But I certainly didn't feel any need for Buddhism in my life. There was no space. I was far to busy, and in any case, my memories of my earlier encounters with Buddhism didn't encourage a favourable response. There was no way that I could envisage that some remote and abstract, philosophy, born out of a wholly different time and place, could help me deal with the kinds of intractable, anxiety-creating, gritty little problems that press in upon all of us, every day of the week. I was prepared to accept that the ideas were interesting and I was quite happy to discuss them over the dinner table. But it simply didn't make sense to suggest to me that chanting, even if I could find the time for such a seemingly vacuous activity, could somehow help me to deal with the bitterness that remained within, and the complex, time-slicing problems that confronted me without; how to be there for the cameras, and yet still be here for my children.

It was a strange and turbulent period, a confused mixture of nascent happiness, and frequent outbursts of anger. By now I thought that I wanted Sarah in my life, as indeed did my children. But I didn't want the Buddhism to which she was now attached. I saw it as an increasingly influential intrusion, a wedge that had come between us. I went to very considerable lengths, lengths that on some occasions even took me by surprise, to dissuade Sarah from continuing with her practice. We argued about it on an almost daily basis. I tried everything that I knew, from reason to ridicule, to dissuade her. There were, as I've said, lots of tears. A few things got broken. The panels in several doors were loosened from being slammed shut so many times, and we came very close to separating. I used to lie awake at night, chasing the problem round and round inside my head. What to do next? Then I had what seemed to me at the time, to be a blinding flash of well…inspiration. I was attacking the problem, I realised, in entirely the wrong way. I was battering at the walls from the outside. All that did was to stiffen Sarah's resolve. What I needed to do was to come at the problem from the *inside* so to speak. I should study this Buddhism in such depth that I would be in a position not to attack it, not at all, but to *reason* it away, to explain coolly and rationally just why it was wholly inappropriate to the sort of life we were living in twentieth century Europe.

If we were playing a game of chess, this was what you might call the Intellectual's Gambit. I devoted considerable amounts of time to studying the Buddhism of Nichiren Daishonin, which is the specific form of Buddhism that Sarah was practising. I read all the books that I could retrieve from Sarah's bookshelves, without her knowledge, and just about anything that I could find in the bibliographies at the back.

The plain fact is that I got a great deal of pleasure out of the process of study. Although I had something of a television reputation for being a sort of action man, I am naturally studious, and Buddhist philosophy is undoubtedly fascinating, since it is about us, about human beings, about how we function and relate to one another. In a sense the study took on a life of its own. It became an end in itself. I read everywhere, on planes and trains, in taxis and buses, and on location between scenes, for hours on end. Buddhist philosophy has been well described somewhere as perhaps the greatest creation of the human mind. It has also evolved in a myriad directions over the past 2500 years, so it is scarcely surprising that there is much in it that I found confusing and contradictory The Lotus Sutra itself ranks alongside The Bible and the Koran as one of *the* great religious texts in the history of mankind, but it is not a read for the fainthearted. It doesn't present its wisdom to anyone, let alone the beginner, on a plate. It is beautiful and full of poetic imagery, but it is also full of immensely obscure language, strange mystical events, and unusual characters.

I'm not at all sure therefore, how effective the intellectual journey had been, but almost without my being aware of it, there had clearly been a substantial spiritual journey as well. The arguments didn't go away, not at all. If anything they became more frequent because I knew so much more, and therefore had more to challenge. But they weren't so filled with anger. Nor were they anything like so destructive. In fact I began to realize that the arguments had subtly changed in character. They had become as it were, a process of exploration, rather than the progressive dismantling that I had envisaged. Sarah was practising if anything more strongly. Moreover, almost without being aware of the healing process, I had become more 'normalised.' Suddenly I found myself going to the theatre and concerts and galleries again and enjoying the fact of being alive.

This process, this journey of exploration went on for about two years. At the end of it I made the decision that I would become a practising Buddhist myself. That may well seem to the outside observer a strange and even inexplicable change, given the strength of my earlier rejection of Buddhism. But perhaps the most surprising thing for me personally, was that it *didn't* seem to be so profound a change after all. Indeed it seemed to have a certain inevitability about it. I didn't feel that I had been required to make some great leap of faith out into the unknown. When I look back at that time, there is no clear memory of intense struggle or inner debate. It was as if I had been on this gradual journey towards understanding. That is not to say that the scepticism was entirely dispelled. Not at all. Scepticism is a tough and resourceful fighter. It doesn't give in easily, and it is very accustomed to putting together bitter rearguard actions.

I still had very strong feelings of negativity and doubt about some of the basic elements of the practice, the process of repetitive chanting for example, and the daily chanting of chapters from the Lotus Sutra. Repetitive chanting is an alien practice in the West. But it is not simply that it is alien. Meditation is cool. Film stars do it. But in general its true to say that chanting is held to have a sort of mindless quality. It is as if one is putting the restless brain into neutral for a while, which is regarded with no little suspicion in an age that is dominated by the power of the intellect. In a sense of course that is very much part of the purpose of chanting. Its role, if I may put it that way, is to cut us free, however briefly, from the overwhelming dominance of the intellectual process per se, to allow other levels of the consciousness, other elements of our inner resource, to come through. For month after month I found myself constantly glancing at the clock while I was chanting, aching for the minutes to tick away more quickly. I was going through the motions, almost out of a sense of obligation, although quite to whom I owed the obligation I wasn't sure. It was a long time before I was able relax into the moment and into the sound, and just allow it to flow through me. Even then I rarely chanted when we had guests staying with us or when we were staying at other peoples houses. And I avoided talking about my practice to other people at the studios or when we were on location. I kept it very much to myself. I was I suppose a sort of "closet Buddhist," and I wasn't ready to come out. I wasn't at all sure where it was taking me, and I wasn't therefore, prepared to reveal it as part of my life. As I've said earlier, no one wants to seem weird to his friends.

And then there were the meetings. I found the monthly discussion meetings for example, quite an ordeal. Basically groups of Buddhists who live locally, get together to discuss some everyday issue from a Buddhist perspective. I didn't want to be part of a group to start with. We are all of us so concerned these days about retaining the distinctive edge of our individuality that we often see challenges where they don't exist. That was true of my experience of these meetings. All I could allow myself to see was that they were unstructured, and aimless, going almost anywhere except towards some sort of meaningful conclusion. It was some time before I was able to slow down, and to shrug off my impatience, so that I could begin to experience these meetings for what they were.

Once I had set my ego to one side in this way it rapidly became clear that in fact, these group meetings provided an immensely valuable forum. They made it possible for all kinds of people, from widely different backgrounds and fields of experience, to share absolutely down-to-earth and everyday experiences, both joyful and painful, in a wholly supportive environment. They were non-judgemental. That was their great quality, and their structure was almost perfect for the task. They enabled people to develop and demonstrate their individuality, because there was no threat. People who at first found it difficult to express themselves in public learned how to do so with some ease and even fluency. You could see people learning how to dig down into their own personal experiences to share them with others, and developing the courage to accept the quite different perspectives that other people might offer. Its not easy, either to talk publicly about one's personal issues, or to have the compassion to share constructively in other people's emotional problems. Both are skills we have to learn, and these meetings provided a forum in which just about anybody could go through that learning process, without threat. Over the weeks and months you could see newcomers join the group, and then begin to change and grow and develop in a quite remarkable way. Essentially these meetings are about people learning together how to put their Buddhism into practice in their daily lives. People had set out on a journey, their lives were moving.

But that is somewhat telescoping my personal experience. For the first year or so I have to say the practice was a real struggle. I pressed on with it really out of a commitment to myself more than anything. As I saw it then, I couldn't point to any marked change in any aspect of my life. That's partly of course because it is simply impossible to monitor life changes in that way. It's rather like watching a tree grow. On a daily basis there is not the slightest discernable difference. Look back after a year and the growth is obvious. But why did I continue? If I look back now it was partly because I had committed myself to it, and I simply wasn't prepared to give up so easily. There seemed no point otherwise. I was determined that once I had set out I would continue on this journey until I was sure one way or the other, about the value of this practice in my daily life.

If I was looking for anything it was that. I was not in any way seeking some grand overarching philosophical view of life that Buddhism might provide. Not that it wasn't there of course, but the fact is that we rarely live our lives at the level of grand strategy. We live in the fine detail of moment to moment, the moment of this happiness or that anxiety. And although it was easy enough for people to say to me, and they did quite frequently, "Buddhism *is* daily life," the question was, did it actually work at that level? Did it work in the unending daily-ness of life; the constant, incoherent, kaleidoscopic stream of incidents and events and encounters that makes up our lives in a modern society? Did it make a fundamental difference to the way one views and deals with the stuff of life? I profoundly wanted it to. My concern was that it couldn't deliver.

The second reason was more inward. I felt, for perhaps the first time in my life, that I was in touch with something that could allow my real self to emerge. That may seem a somewhat obscure thing to say, but the fact is, that like many people, I had developed a very strong set of defences to maintain the absolute privacy of what I thought of as my inner life. Although I had a strong emotional life, my deepest feelings were for my eyes only. I lived my life behind this outer wall. I was deeply concerned about what people thought of me, and I was extremely well practised at presenting to this audience or that, only what seemed to *me*, to be appropriate to them.

Or at least I thought I was, but of course we are very skilled at reading the character behind the wall. Although I'm sure that many people, men perhaps more commonly than women, live much of their lives behind this sort of defensive barricade. The real William didn't often stand up for all to see, and if I am completely honest, I think that was true even for my immediate family, my brothers and my sisters. Only my children, and my Sarah, sat within my innermost defences.

But with my Buddhist practice I felt an emerging sense of freedom and of optimism. I felt that I could reveal my true self, openly and freely, and it didn't matter what people thought as long as I was true to myself. That is a wonderful feeling. That sense of emerging freedom became immensely important to me. It was the basis, I came to realize, of a strong underlying sense of well being. What had seemed like no change, had in fact been a time of the quite profound change. The tree had flourished. I was enjoying life, and being among people. It was not that anything had changed in the essential nature of life. How could it? The inescapable nature of human life is that it is pretty much a succession of challenges of one kind or another. The difficulties and the problems hadn't gone away. In my case, if anything they had increased. The family was still living through the aftershocks of a very painful divorce, and added to that there were very considerable financial strains because of the dip in my career among other things. But despite those problems, which were there on a daily basis, I didn't feel weighed down or over-burdened. The panic had gone. So too had the wearying anxiety, to be replaced by this emerging sense of stability that came, at least in part I thought, from the daily Buddhist practice. I had this strong underlying sense that I was climbing out of the hole.

CHAPTER THREE

Where did it Come From?

The extraordinary fact is that over the past 40 years or so, perhaps a little longer, many tens of thousands of people in Europe and the Americas who have been brought up and lived their lives in an essentially Judaeo-Christian culture, have chosen to adopt a set of practices and beliefs that come from a completely different, some might even say an alien culture. It is quite difficult to find a historical parallel for that sort of spontaneous movement, on that scale.

One could reasonably argue I think that Europe became Christian largely because of the existence of the Roman Empire. Jesus and St. Paul, his primary missionary, happened to be alive at the time when the Roman Empire was expanding to embrace the whole of Western Europe. The Empire gave Christianity a focal point, Rome, and a highly developed infrastructure to carry the news of Christianity to its furthest corners. That settled the destiny of Europe for the next 2000 years. Europe became dominated by the Christian Church, and Christianity was carried overseas by the Spanish and Portuguese and British traders and settlers wherever they went, religion that is, spread both by the sword and by fervent missionaries. The effect is that the whole of the New World, and those areas of the Old that were settled by the European newcomers, effectively became part of the Judaeo-Christian world.

Buddhism, from its origins in Northern India in the 5th Century BCE, didn't flow westwards. It went eastwards; south and east into present day Sri Lanka and Thailand and Vietnam, north and east through Tibet and China and Korea to Japan.

Now, and essentially for the first time in its 2500 year history, Buddhism is flowing westwards, out of Japan and Asia, into Europe and the Americas, and it is travelling not on the backs of missionaries but essentially by word of mouth. Person speaking to person.

Indeed the fact is that never in its history has Buddhism spread so widely and so rapidly, in terms of geographical area, and never before in the religious history of the West, have so many people turned to Buddhism, to seek answers to their questions about life, the universe and everything. There are no easy answers to explain this process. The people who have adopted this Buddhist practice come from all walks of life, all kinds of backgrounds, all kinds of careers; butchers and bakers and candlestick makers. And lawyers and taxi drivers and plumbers and writers. Ordinary people, living in the real world, doing a job, falling in love, bringing up children, caring for elderly relatives, worried about the mortgage or the tax bill or achieving the next promotion or whatever, and choosing to put it all together within the framework of Buddhism. It is, in itself, a remarkable revolution.

What makes it perhaps all the more remarkable is that in an age that is driven by rampant materialism and widespread cynicism, and marked by plummeting church attendances, this practice is not an easy touch. It is genuinely demanding. It calls for constant application and effort because you are learning new skills and fundamentally new ways of thinking about yourself and how to tackle the problems that are inherent in all our daily lives.

An extremely interesting observation was made recently by a senior religious figure, a Christian Bishop as it happens, as part of a discussion on the place of religion in today's society. He observed that traditionally, in the West, people have sought the expression of their deepest spirituality within the established forms of religion. That has been the situation for many centuries. But his view was that for several decades now, and particularly during recent years, people still seek the experience of their spirituality, but they want it without the structure and the 'restriction' of formalised religion. They want, that is, the sense of liberation that comes from experiencing their spirituality directly, in their own person, free from the formalities that are so much a part of established churches. That observation is, I think, a genuine insight. It offers at least a partial explanation perhaps, for the fact that Buddhism has spread so rapidly and so widely in the West, because it answers very closely to that modern need, for tens of thousands, or indeed, if we include Japan, the many millions of people around the world who have chosen to base their lives upon this practice. A practice that presents us with an all-embracing vision of the way the world works, but without dogma and prescription, and that places immense emphasis on individual responsibility for both practice and action.

Shakyamuni Buddha

All Buddhist teachings stem essentially from Shakyamuni's life experience. He is the root from which this great tree has grown. His teachings have changed the course of world history. But he lived a long time ago, when nothing was written down, so much has become obscured, and, as you would expect, it is often difficult to distinguish between historical fact and the myths and legends that have grown up around so large a life.

Shakyamuni himself didn't claim any kind of divine connection. He was rooted firmly in this world. He was born the son of the ruler of the Shakya tribe or clan, hence the name Shakya-muni, or *"Sage of the Shakyas."* This small, semi-autonomous kingdom lay on the borders of modern-day Nepal. The closest modern research can get is to place his birth between the 5th and 6th centuries BCE. The precise date may not be important but the period is, because within the space of little more than 100 years, a remarkable number of great seminal thinkers, were creating an extraordinary tide of revolutionary ideas about the nature of human life, right across the known world, from Socrates in Greece, and Isaiah in Palestine, to Confucius in China, and Shakyamuni in Northern India.

As a result this period of immense intellectual ferment has been described as the dawn of our spiritual civilisation; the brief period that produced virtually all the ideas that have driven man's spiritual history from then right up until the beginning of the era of science and technology in the late 19th Century.

Shakyamuni, as the eldest son would have been groomed to take over this kingdom from his father at some stage, and he seems to have lived a life of some seclusion in his father's palace, having little contact with the world of poverty and hardship of the people outside. Apart from that he seems to have pursued what in most respects was an ordinary, if somewhat affluent life. He married around the age of 16 and had a son, who later became one of his leading disciples. But Shakyamuni was clearly no ordinary man. Quite suddenly, when he was in his late 20s according to the most widely accepted tradition, Shakyamuni decided to abandon the life pattern that had been established for him, and leave his father's house and family. He committed himself from then on to a religious life, to the search for truth; a decision made by one man, in a small town in Northern India, that has profoundly affected the lives of many millions of people down the centuries.

What was it that drove him to make such a radical departure? Although unusual, it was not a wholly unprecedented event. It seems that eldest sons in privileged households in Northern India at this time, might well decide to pursue the path of truth, or enlightenment, rather than follow in their fathers footsteps into a political or commercial career. In Shakyamuni's case, tradition provides us with a very clear motivation. It seems that when he became aware of the sheer scale of the suffering and hardship of ordinary men and women in the real world outside the walls of the palace, he found the experience so overwhelming that he simply couldn't ignore it. He was driven to take some action, to do something about it, to save mankind if you like. More or less immediately he gave up everything he had. He left his family and he set off essentially to find some way of transcending or dealing with, the sufferings that are inherent in human life.

The story of just how he became aware of the extent of human suffering is told in the form of a myth or a legend that has such a key role to play in Buddhist teachings that it has to be repeated here. It is known as the four encounters or the four sufferings.

Shakyamuni is said to have gone out of the palace gates into the small town of Kapilavastu where it was situated, on four separate occasions. When he went out by the East Gate he met a man who was scarcely able to hobble along, bent over and crippled with age. Going out of the Southern Gate he met someone who was very sick. From the West Gate he saw a corpse being carried away. Emerging from the North Gate he encountered what was a common phenomenon then, a religious ascetic seeking the answer to the riddle of human existence through extreme physical deprivation.

Myth, or legend, or the formalised account of some real event we cannot know. Certainly real life rarely occurs in such neat and regular patterns. But this account, however formalised, undoubtedly serves to focus the attention, once heard never forgotten, on the heart of the matter. The essential starting point of the Buddhist religion is the mystery or the dilemma of human suffering; the problems of old age, sickness and death, together with birth, or the fact of living itself. They represent here, swiftly and graphically, the fundamental questions of human existence. What is human life about? What gives rise to human suffering? How can we best deal with it?

They are questions that challenge us just as powerfully today of course. We may choose not to look at them, or not to recognize them, particularly if we happen to be in the midst of our youthful life, but as Job reminds us, whatever stage in the journey we are at, we can't escape them, *"Man is born to troubles as the sparks fly upwards"* he reminds us. Indeed it could well be argued that man invented religion, in his own image so to speak, to cope with the eternal problem of pain and suffering in this life.

It helps as well to understand something about the environment into which Shakyamuni went, to pursue his search for clearer answers to the human condition. He was born and grew up in a society that was traditionally dominated by a Brahman priestly class, which wielded an almost divine authority. They did so as the representatives on earth of a powerful pantheon of gods who ruled over all the affairs of men. To avoid the wrath of the gods was a daily concern for everyone, at every level.

He will also have been aware of new and powerful forces stirring in the world outside. Forces that were beginning to break the patterns of the older tribal society, built around centuries of this Brahman religious authority. There was a huge increase in commerce and trade in northern India, leading to the rise of a new, rich and powerful merchant class, and the growth of larger towns and cities. People began to move in considerable numbers from the close knit and rural communities, bound by ancient traditions, into the richer towns and cities, where family and tribal ties were looser. So there were the first beginnings of a rootless, disconnected urban society. Above all, the religious and intellectual authority of the Brahman priestly class, that had underpinned the social structure for centuries, was being openly challenged. Ordinary people were seeking greater freedoms.

Shakyamuni spent several years in what might be called his personal wilderness. Travelling his own inner journey. Going though his own process of spiritual evolution and development. At the same time he explored what were held then, and indeed now to some extent, to be the most successful routes towards enlightenment, or the deepest understanding of life.

I don't think that this should surprise us in any way. Even the greatest revolutionaries are to some extent prisoners of their time, and the conventional routes to self-knowledge were held to be meditation and asceticism. So Shakyamuni studied with two of the most highly respected teachers in yogic meditation, until he himself had attained their level of awakening or concentration; *"the place where nothing exists,"* as it has been described. Then he departed, realising, according to the Buddhist texts that describe this part of his life, that these kinds of practices, taken to the extreme, led to a kind of emptiness. They had little to offer the ordinary person trying to eke out an existence in a tough and challenging world. They had become in a sense a cul de sac, an end in themselves. They led not so much to a better way of life, but only to *"the place where nothing exists."*

When the advanced practices of yoga had failed him Shakyamuni moved on to a period of the most severe ascetic practices or "austerities" as they were called, involving acts like prolonged fasting and suspension of breathing, almost to the point of death. If the body weighs down the spirit, and blocks the progress of the mind towards spiritual enlightenment, then in some way that bond must be broken. This sort of thinking is not of course restricted to ancient Brahmanism. It is with us today in several forms. Indeed many people will recognize an element of this sort of dualism, of the mind-body conflict, in some forms of modern Christianity.

Shakyamuni clearly believed that he had to taste the pain and the anguish of deep suffering if he were to grasp the meaning of spiritual freedom. He tested these forms of extreme self-denial to the very limit, before he was prepared to accept that this also was not the path to the liberation of the spirit that he was seeking. Essentially he realized that these punishing practices were simply wrecking his body and limiting rather than heightening his ability to think clearly or take positive action. He gave them up, he began to build up his debilitated body again, and he began to meditate.

Shakyamunis Enlightenment

What happened to Shakyamuni under the Bodhi tree, near the village of Buddhagaya, during his long period of meditation is hard to understand and even harder to describe, in a way that makes it wholly accessible to the modern inquirer. We can't understand it, any more than we can understand what really happened to the Christian persecutor Saul on the road to Damascus that turned him into St Paul, the greatest missionary and architect of the Christian Church. These moments of extreme revelation or enlightenment in certain individual's lives, that go on to change the whole direction of human history, are, by definition, rare and deeply mystical in the truest sense of that word. They are genuinely beyond the reach of the intellect.

In many ways the concept of a state of being, or a state of mind labelled "enlightenment" is strange, not to say alien to us. It is a word we are not likely to use very often, if at all. In an essentially intellectual and materialist age we are much more attuned to, and much more comfortable with, matter-of-fact explanations and scientific patterns of proof, than we are with mystical experiences. But of course, as we all know, there is much more to our humanity than can be observed in a laboratory. We have to accept, I think, that in using an unusual word like "enlightenment," we are reaching out in an attempt to describe something that may be difficult to pin down, but which remains nonetheless, a wholly valid part of human experience.

Shakyamuni, rather like Jesus who came long after, taught in the oral tradition. Nothing was written down. It was only many years after his death that his followers came together to create a written collection of his teachings, which were numbered in their thousands. In his book *The Living Buddha,* Daisaku Ikeda explains how the accounts in early Buddhist scriptures describe Shakyamuni's enlightenment as a *"state of perfect and unsurpassed wisdom."*

But what does that mean for us? Many attempts have been made to bring the implications of that experience closer for us, and they contain many elements that have become the central pillars of Buddhism, the ideas that underlie the entire structure; above all perhaps, the profound interconnectedness between all things in the universe, from the dust between our toes to the galaxies out at the edge of space, and the understanding that change, or impermanence or entropy perhaps, to use a more scientific term, is the very nature of all things. Nothing ever stays the same from one moment to the next. Everything that is or was, going through the same endless cycle of birth, growth, decline and death.

Becoming, growing, subsiding, dying.

Formation, continuation, decline, disintegration.

The only variable is the period of the cycle, from a few milliseconds for the sub atomic particle, to the life span of a human being, or a tree, or a mountain, and on to the many millions of years encompassing the life cycle of a star from birth to its decline and death. They all become, grow, decline and die.

And yet, paradoxically, underlying that cycle of flux and change, there is this single constancy, the constancy of the *rhythm* itself, that sustains and supports the endlessly repeated stages of the cycle from birth to death. What Nichiren Buddhism calls the Universal or the Mystic Law. There's that word mystic again, beyond the reach of the intellect alone.

Whatever the precise nature of the truths that Shakyamuni perceived, whatever elements of the story we find difficult to believe or to understand, the essential point to hang onto is that the immense, moving power of this experience lit a fire in Shakyamuni that was never extinguished. It launched him into a lifetime of endeavour from which he was never able to pull back, even to the very moment of his death. Just like St. Paul after his experience on the road to Damascus, Shakyamuni was never again able to separate his existence as a human being, from his teaching of the truths that he had experienced. He spoke of it literally until his last breath. Today we all inhabit a different world because of the experiences that Shakyamuni went through at Buddhagaya and the fire that it lit within him, never to be extinguished. It continues to reach out to us over the vast gap of time that intervenes. I am writing these words because of that experience, and my young son Sebastian chants before he goes to school in the morning because of that experience.

It created in Shakyamuni an up welling of joy, and of compassion for all of humankind so powerful, that, again, rather like

St Paul, it never deserted him. He was tireless in his efforts to find the ways to convey the essence of what he had learned in terms that made a *practical* difference to ordinary people's lives. Central to that teaching was the message that the wisdom and the perceptions that he had received, although they were clearly mystical, they were not in any sense divine or alien to ordinary human existence. How could they be, since he was no more, nor no less than that, an ordinary human being. They were simply the highest reach of an ordinary human mind.

When I read his words I have to say that they strongly evoke for me the image of a Ghandi-like figure. Certainly like Ghandi, Shakyamuni must have been a man of great charisma and a teacher of immense authority. He didn't teach enlightenment so much as he taught healing, and hope, how to cope with day to day difficulties, how to handle sickness and despair, or anger and alienation. He taught always at a level that could be received and comprehended by his audience, since his teachings were radical in the extreme, particularly when seen against the centuries-long background of Brahmanism.

Throughout the long period of his teaching he steadily evolved and deepened this powerful humanistic philosophy and he gained many millions of followers from all walks of life, from street beggars to merchants and from craftsmen to kings. Before his death however he predicted that although his teachings would go on spreading widely and have great influence for many hundreds of years, they would eventually begin to lose their ability to help ordinary people, during a period of great confusion and conflict that he called "The Latter day of the Law." But out of the confusion he predicted a great new teaching would appear based upon his own ultimate teaching, The Lotus Sutra.

The Early Spread of Buddhism

After Shakyamuni's death his teachings, offering a radically new approach to life, and a new kind of hope and optimism available to everyone, spread like a bushfire eastwards throughout South East Asia. As with any great body of thought it became subject to differing interpretations and practice, and quite early in the history of Buddhism, two great rivers of Buddhist practice developed. The stream of Buddhism that spread   south and east into Sri Lanka and Thailand and South East Asia, was based largely on some of the earlier teachings of Shakyamuni, that he himself had called "provisional," given his avowed purpose of taking people with him on a spiritual journey, slowly evolving and deepening their understanding.

This South Eastern stream of Buddhism, is called Theravada or Hinayana Buddhism; Theravada meaning essentially "Teaching of the Elders." It has a marked tendency towards monasticism, with immensely detailed codes of observance, often so detailed that only those who are prepared to take up the monastic life can have the time to follow them to the letter. It is also renowned in parts of South East Asia for its ornate temples, often with large gilt statues of the Buddha. In *The Buddha in Daily Life* Richard Causton has characterised Hinayana or Theravada Buddhism as follows,

'This is probably the form of Buddhism best known in the West; for some it has even created the impression that Buddhism involves the worship of idols. Moreover, since the application of Hinayana Buddhism to daily life is limited, its appeal to date has been mainly as a subject for academic study. This has naturally

tended to reinforce the idea...that Buddhism is primarily concerned with intellectual abstraction, a means of escaping from the material side of life into a 'higher reality' through various forms of physical and mental discipline.'

The other main river of Buddhism flowed North and West, through Tibet and into China, around the beginning of the Christian era, and eventually to Korea and Japan. This stream of Buddhism, called Mahayana, places great emphasis on carrying Buddhist teachings into the lives of ordinary people living in the secular world. Indeed Mahayana translates as 'The Greater Vehicle' making clear that its purpose is to carry all people towards a higher state of life.

A key point to hold onto is that the central text of Mahayana Buddhism is the Lotus Sutra. Sutra means teaching, while the lotus of the title is seen to be a powerful metaphor for many things, one of the most important being that since it is a plant that grows in a muddy swampy environment, and yet produces the most beautiful of flowers, it is symbolic of the great potential locked up in the mundane travail of human life. This long sutra, filled with extraordinary images and metaphors and parable-like stories was the mainspring of Shakyamuni's mission during the last 10 years or so of his life, and is described as representing the very core and essence of his life's work. It alone explains his most fundamental insight, namely that each and every one of us has the inherent potential for Buddhahood. Although, as he himself was only too well aware, the message of the Lotus Sutra was by no means an easy one for ordinary people to absorb, or believe in, then or now. As he says in the Lotus Sutra itself;

"Among all the sutras that I have preached, now preach and will

*preach, The Lotus Sutra is the most difficult to believe in and the most difficult to understand."**

Many people are troubled to some extent by the sheer number of Buddhist schools, although of course, we are quite accustomed to the fact that a fracturing into different groupings is a feature of all the major world religions, Christianity, Judaism, Islam and Hinduism alike. It would seem almost inevitable that wherever you have a great body of thought that seeks to explain the immense complexities of life, it will be open to differing interpretations, at different times and in different locations. In that sense it is doing no more than mirror the complexity of the life that it is seeking to illuminate, and should be seen as a richness rather than as a confusion.

Nichiren Daishonin

One of the greatest and most controversial teachers, who had a major role to play in the evolution and transmission of Buddhist teachings to the modern world, was born in 1222, in a little fishing village on the Southern coast of Japan. He lived for 60 years. He spent virtually all of his life, almost from his boyhood, immersed in study and teaching, and yet reaching out in exactly the same way as Shakyamuni had, to ordinary people. He also had the courage to take on the military junta, the military dictatorship that ruled in Japan at the time, over its abuse of power and neglect of the common people of Japan. He became known as The Great Sage, or Nichiren Daishonin.

Nichiren went into a monastery when he was 12, essentially because a monastery was about the only place at that time where a boy could learn to read and write. Apart from that he was an ordinary boy who had an ordinary upbringing,

although clearly, from a very early age he had unusual qualities of perception, and courage and compassion. Early on in
his life he became strongly aware of two things that he
believed were closely inter-linked. One was the scale of
conflict and the depths of suffering that dominated the lives
of ordinary people in 13th Century Japan. The second was the
great confusion of teachings that was represented by the
sheer range of Buddhist schools. Ordinary people he realised,
didn't know what to believe in or how to practice. Since at that
time, religious practice played a dominant role in everyone's
life, the inner confusion was reflected in the widespread levels
of pain and suffering and conflict in ordinary people's lives.

As young as he was, Nichiren Daishonin essentially committed his life at that point, to sorting out this confusion, a situation that is strangely reminiscent of the decision taken so
many centuries earlier by Shakyamuni. That early vow led to
his becoming the most persistent and outspoken religious
and social reformer of his day. He was utterly fearless. No
threats, no promises of punishment by the authorities
deterred him. He became a priest at the age of 16 and devoted
the next 15 years, his entire youth, to a personal quest to
unravel the confusion in Buddhist teachings, travelling round
the leading monasteries in Japan, which were the reposito-
ries of the ancient transcripts of the Buddhist texts. In this
way he painstakingly traced the golden thread of Buddhist
thought back through Japanese and Chinese and Indian
writings to Shakyamuni himself... and to the Lotus Sutra.

The result of Nichiren Daishonin's quest essentially
launched the modern revolution in Mahayana Buddhism.
The extraordinary fact is that it is really only in the past 50
years or so, with the post- war liberalisation and opening
up of Japanese society, that Nichiren Buddhism has begun

to spread around the world. Fundamentally, he re-established what had become completely obscured in the proliferation of Buddhist sects, namely the primacy of the Lotus Sutra as the heart of Shakyamuni's message.

But Nichiren went much further than any other Buddha before him. From the depths of his own enlightenment and his profound understanding of human nature, he revealed, or created an immensely simple, down-to-earth method by which all ordinary people could begin to practice Buddhism regardless of the demands pressing in upon them in their daily lives. That was his immense contribution, creating a model of Buddhist practice that is accessible to ordinary people then and now; accessible to people today for example, living busy, active, time-slicing lives in a modern society. That is one of the reasons no doubt, why he is sometimes called the Buddha for the Modern Age.

With this essentially simple daily practice Nichiren revealed in a sense the ultimate Mahayana vehicle that so many people had been seeking for so long; powerful, undoubtedly mystical, and yet utterly accessible to everybody. For the very first time here was a method to enable all people without exception, young and old, men and women, rich or poor, philosopher and labourer, to fold a meaningful and life-enhancing Buddhist practice into their daily lives. It was a major milestone in the history of Buddhism, indeed in the history of religion. Nichiren Daishonin lived and taught in 13th Century Japan, but his vision was timeless, aimed at all of humanity down the centuries.

Historically speaking, Nichiren, very like Shakyamuni before him, was a profound social reformer. He was born into a rigidly feudal society, ruled by a powerful military dictatorship within which various sectarian priesthoods had immense influence over the detail of the lives of ordinary people. Women had virtually no rights. Yet here he was openly preaching a Buddhism that spoke of the universality of Buddhahood for all, men and women alike, respect for the individual whatever his or her status in society, and the potential for all men to lead a life free from suffering. It was heady stuff and inevitably he became a marked man; feared by the priests of the schools he attacked and defeated in debate, persecuted by the military shogunate whose approach to government he sought to reform.

He spent his life clarifying the essence of Shakyamuni's teachings and helping ordinary people to see their Buddhism as wholly practical, not a thing apart, but part of the fabric of their daily experience. He wrote to them constantly, supporting and guiding them, through countless everyday problems; everyday then and just as everyday now, from an argument with an employer, to anxiety over a sick child or grief at the death of a husband. Always the message is the positive one of hope and optimism, always seeking to deepen their grasp of the strange paradox that lies at the very heart of Buddhism; that suffering is inevitable in our lives, but it is also the *essential* platform on which we build the strength and the resilience to experience happiness. He taught that when we are weak our problems seem huge, even overwhelming. When we are strong the problems appear to shrink in size. The essential issue therefore is not how to eliminate problems from one's life, which is a delusion, but how to grow stronger. And there is really only one way to achieve that ...by overcoming problems.

When Nichiren died at the age of 60, his legacy was huge. He had created a teaching and a practice that has the potential not only to transform an individual approach to life, but it has the reach and the capacity to transform from the bottom up, the way modern societies work.

Nichiren Buddhism in Today's World

The historical thread that links Nichiren Daishonin's teaching in medieval Japan, to the remarkable growth and interest in his teachings around the world today, is a story of extraordinary drama. After Nichiren's death his teaching remained locked up in a feudal Japan that was virtually closed off and isolated from the rest of the world. It was sustained within a relatively small population of priests and practitioners, passing it on from generation to generation. That is in itself a remarkable story. Then, in the 20th century two key events occurred. The first was in the 1920's when a determined and visionary Japanese educator named Makiguchi, dedicated to social reform through changes in the educational system, found in Nichiren's teachings the powerful philosophical basis he had been seeking for a wholly new approach to education in Japan. He was aware of educational developments in the West and he wanted to turn Japan away from the impersonal, learning-by-rote regimentation that characterised its educational system, to establish an approach that sought the development of each student's individual potential. In 1930 he set up a society with these radical aims, based firmly upon Nichiren Buddhism. This gradually developed over the following decade into a wider movement of people who both practised and spread the principles of Nichiren Buddhism in Japanese society.

With the rise to power of the military Junta in Japan in the 1930's this small but intensely liberal and progressive organisation was seen to be something of a threat to the widespread promotion of a nationwide form of worship,

Shintoism, dedicated to the support of the Junta's far-reaching military ambitions. Makiguchi, and his closest follower, a man called Josei Toda, were imprisoned because they refused to give up their beliefs. Makiguchi died in prison in 1944, prepared to give up his life literally for his beliefs. Josei Toda was released in 1945, emaciated and unwell, his health permanently damaged by his ordeal in captivity.

But he had never for a moment given up his practice, and it had clearly created in him an indomitable inner strength. He was released into a totally different world. Japan had been crushed, and much of its infrastructure had been destroyed. Many of its cities were in ruins. In 1945 General MacArthur was made supreme ruler in Japan for a period of some 5 years with complete powers to oversee the reconstruction of the country and to introduce a raft of liberal measures that were to transform Japanese society; measures as radical in that still feudal country as equality for women, freedom of education and complete freedom of religion.

The time found the man. From what must have been the lowest point in his own life, and the life of the Japanese people, Josei Toda somehow found within himself the strength and the inspiration to set out once again. He began to talk publicly about Nichiren Buddhism with its clearly defined methods of practice, and its message of hope, and courage, and down-to-earth solutions for the problems of everyday existence. To a people who had been crushed by the long years of military dictatorship, and overwhelmed by the devastation that fire bombs and nuclear bombs had wrought on their cities, it was a message that lifted them above their despair. Within 10 years there were many thousands of people who had come to base their lives on the principles of Nichiren Buddhism.

Today, the organization originally founded by Makiguchi, now called the SGI, or Soka Gakkai International (Soka means 'value creating' and Gakkai means 'society') has spread around the world. It owes much to its remarkable leader over the past half century, Daisaku Ikeda, who is one of the greatest thinkers and writers on Buddhism in the modern world. He has travelled the world and worked tirelessly for several decades to spread the message of Nichiren Buddhism, both as a solid basis for individual lives, and as a major vehicle for peace and reconciliation in a conflict-ridden World.

The SGI is very much an enabling organization. It is in many ways like a global university, in that it provides a structure within which, entirely at their own pace and in their own way, people of many nations and widely different cultural backgrounds, can study Buddhism and its implications, both for their own lives and the wider working of society. To this end the SGI translates, and publishes and issues commentaries and observations and arranges seminars and study sessions and debates. It is wholly voluntary in all its activities. You seek it out, rather than it seeking you. Through its mediation some 15 million people today, from every conceivable background and culture and way of life, have chosen to base their lives on Nichiren Buddhism.

But what precisely does it mean, to base one's life on Nichiren Buddhism?

Chapter Four

A Question of Faith

Faith is a word that clearly travels with a lot of baggage, gathered over the long centuries of religious tradition. But what can it possibly mean, you might ask, in a religion that has no gods to have faith in?

In all the major religions with which we are most familiar, or which we encounter on our travels, in all the Abrahamic religions for example, Christianity, Judaism and Islam, faith is, in a sense, the glue, the matrix, that holds together those elements of the teaching that are beyond the reach of proof. As you would expect with any religion that has to deal with the nature of divinity itself, and the unknowable afterlife, faith has an immense role to play, since those unproveable elements are substantial.

So, basically, wherever a religious doctrine cannot be validated by human experience, then it becomes, by definition, a question of faith. Essentially that comes to mean, believe in this teaching or this piece of doctrine, because God or the wisdom of the church has declared it to be so. That Jesus was the Son of God, for example, born of a virgin birth, and that he ascended into heaven and sits on the right hand of God the Father. Or that in the central Christian principle of the Trinity, the son *is* actually the father. Or that Muhammad received the words of the Quran, dictated directly by the Angel Jibril. The believer is called upon to make what we have come to call a leap of faith, to accept that element of the doctrine.

The use of that familiar word "leap" in this context is accurate, in that it truly indicates what we have to do. The believer is leaving the comfort and assurance of solid ground, you might say, and trusting himself to something well beyond his normal experience. That is not of course suggesting that such a leap of faith is necessarily difficult. Clearly it isn't, given the sustained and hugely sustaining power of Christianity and Islam for many millions of people down the centuries. Once again I must make it clear that in no way is this to be interpreted as a value judgement. Not in any way. I am simply seeking to understand differences in the way in which we use this key word, faith, and in all these major religions, faith is clearly much to do with the belief in the power of God or Allah, and the role of that power in human lives.

What do we do however when we come to Buddhism? Since there is no all-powerful creator God in Buddhism, the word faith must carry a very different meaning, and it is clearly important that we try to grasp for ourselves what that meaning is.

The fundamental difference we learn right from the outset, in Nichiren Buddhism, is that faith is not in any way to be equated with belief in something *outside* of oneself. In fact Buddhist texts make this point absolutely clear. As Nichiren express it, we have to look for it within.

*"Your practice of the Buddhist teachings will not relieve you of the sufferings of birth and death in the least unless you perceive the true nature of your life. If you seek enlightenment outside yourself, then your performing even ten thousand practices and ten thousand good deeds will be in vain. It is like the case of the poor man who spends night and day counting his neighbour's wealth but gains not even half a coin."**

So what might faith mean then, in this context? *"…perceive the true nature of your life,"* we are told.

So the somewhat surprising answer, is that it is essentially about one's belief in *oneself.* It is related to the strength of the desire or the determination *within one's own life,* to act or to live in a particular way. Faith, in Buddhist terms, then, is not dissimilar to the determination or the self-belief with which you might pursue any major goal in your life, to achieve a level of excellence in a profession for example, or in a sporting or artistic career. The fundamental difference, and it is undoubtedly fundamental, is that in this case the self-belief is anchored firmly in a set of teachings that have arisen from Shakyamuni, and been evolved by a series of great thinkers and teachers over the past two and a half thousand years.

In this sense then it seems clear that the Buddhism of Nichiren Daishonin asks you to take part in what might be described as a huge on-going experiment, by putting the claims that it makes to the test, in *your own life.* Summon up from within it says, this self-belief, this determination, take up the practice, follow the steps that it lays down; *"exert yourself, in the ways of practice and study,"* and *observe* the results in your own life, to see whether or not it delivers its promise.

How Can we Test it Out?

Nichiren was undoubtedly a great teacher and philosopher, but he was also immensely practical and down to earth. He chose to live out almost his entire life amongst ordinary farm workers and craftsmen, getting to grips with their daily problems, using Buddhist principles to help them get on with their lives. He was overwhelmingly concerned to demonstrate, in ways that made complete sense to ordinary people, how their daily lives might be improved through an understanding of Buddhist principles and Buddhist practice. Our material circumstances have of course changed immensely since he lived, but our fundamental humanity remains the same. We are, that is to say, pretty much in the same boat, ordinary human beings, with lots of things going on in our lives that present a challenge. Nichiren taught above all that though we cannot change the nature of human life, we can fundamentally change our *attitude* to that life, and it is essentially our attitude to the pains and problems that we encounter, that determines whether or not we can establish happiness at the centre of our lives. That, put simply, is the essence of his teaching, and he knew full well, that it was not an easy teaching for us to take on board.

So Nichiren actually posed the question for us, how are we to judge whether or not his teachings have any validity?

That is a central problem is it not, in a humanistic religion, passed on from one *ordinary* human being to another, rather than being based upon dogma or commandments, handed down with all the authority of a god or a divine creator behind them? The commandments of a god brook no debate you might say. The guidance from another human being demands it.

Right from the start Nichiren recognized that this was a central problem that we all face, now as then, to judge the relevant from the irrelevant, the good teaching from the bad, so he supplied the answer to his question. Don't take it on trust, he said. Look for very clear proof. In fact, look for *three* kinds of proof, in judging or estimating the validity of his teachings, or for that matter any religious or philosophical proposition that we might encounter. And he spelt them out for us. The first of these is what he called the *Documentary proof.* Does it have a solid documentary basis. Something that we can get hold of, and read in order to learn the essential nature of the teaching itself. The books of the Torah for example, or the New Testament, or the Koran, the great books of Hinduism or The Lotus Sutra, represent this kind of proof. The second he called *Theoretical Proof*, or the extent to which the teaching makes sense to us. Is it fantastical and magical, or does it present a view of reality that bears comparison with the process of life as we experience it, and enables us to make greater sense of that reality?

But it is the third proof that Nichiren talks about that really strikes a chord. He calls it the *Actual Proof,* which takes us right back to that fundamental question that was posed earlier, and that underlies just about everything in this journey, namely what is the purpose of a spiritual or a religious belief in our lives? When he is talking about actual proof, Nichiren is talking about the actual effects that we experience in our own lives as a result of our association with this practice. Buddhism actually uses the word, "benefits" to describe these effects. Is the teaching a practical proposition? Does it genuinely help us with things like overcoming our problems or facing up to our challenges. Does it support us, help us to live stronger, more positive, value-creating lives despite all the challenges and anxieties that we are bound to encounter as human beings.

All three kinds of proof are clearly important in relation to any philosophy or religious teaching we encounter, but, Nichiren argues that above all we should regard actual, demonstrable proof of the benefits of any practice in our daily lives as the crucial test of its validity. If you think about it even for a moment, it is *the* fundamental question. Does it work? Does it enhance our everyday lives? That is the question that this practice invites you to ask. It requires nothing that might be described as blind faith. It *does* require the self belief and the determination that we talked of earlier, in order to give it a reasonable chance.

You take note of the doubts and the misgivings about the practice that undoubtedly arise, particularly in the early days, but they can arise at any time, and you ask questions and study more widely in order to seek some resolution of them. But in the final analysis it will not be what you *read*, or what you are *told* about Buddhism that will convince you of its validity, although of course they both have an important part to play. In the end it has to be the gradual accumulation of your own experiences that prove to you that it makes sense in terms of your own life, or not. The practice is too demanding to be continued on the basis of what somebody else tells you about it. The deepening belief in the life-changing power of Buddhism has to come from within, since it in-volves coming to terms with the idea of your own Buddhahood, and in some ways this is perhaps the most difficult step of all.

What do We Mean by Buddhahood?

We are accustomed to thinking of 'the Buddha' as being the great historical figure of Shakyamuni. There have of course been many other Buddhas throughout history, but when we add the article *"the,"* it is undoubtedly Shakyamuni we are identifying. As we have seen, he made no claims to divinity or divine inspiration at any time in his lifetime. Indeed he specifically forbade his followers from making any such connection. However, as a purely historical figure, he clearly occupies a place in western minds *alongside* the other great founders of religion such as Jesus and Mohammed, who *did* of course claim a divine connection. Indeed that was the very basis of their mission on Earth. They claimed to be in their different ways the channel through which divine purpose was transmitted to mankind.

Because of this parallel status, for all intents and purposes we are used to attributing to the title Buddha, if not the very special qualities of divinity, something very close to it. Indeed, in South East Asia, as we have seen, Shakyamuni has been virtually deified, with huge golden statues occupying pride of place in Buddhist temples, and since it was this form of Buddhism that was first encountered and described in the West, this sense of deification, very much colours the western response to the word Buddhahood.

What Me?

It is therefore something of a shock when we first encounter the central teaching of the Lotus Sutra and Nichiren Buddhism, which is that Buddhahood is not a quality possessed by one very special man in history, or even by a very few men down the centuries. Buddhahood, it teaches, is a universal quality inherent in everyone, without exception, part of our essential humanity. It argues that we all have that immense potential within us, whether or not we accept it, or believe in it, or have the slightest interest in understanding what it means. Everyone you sit alongside in the bus, the man you buy your morning newspaper from, all the colleagues you encounter on a daily basis at work. Those you like and those you don't.

Once again, it is unquestionably a huge, life-changing idea. It is nothing less than a revolution in the history of spiritual development. It was part of Shakyamuni's enlightenment, and was revolutionary when he first expounded it in the Lotus Sutra. It was still revolutionary when Nichiren Daishonin taught it in 13th century Japan. It remains revolutionary today, in the sense of being a very difficult idea to understand or to believe in and to act upon, as the central inspiration for living through all the mundane muddle of our daily lives.

That, in essence, is what the daily Buddhist practice is all about, helping us to move along that path of understanding, and *folding* that understanding into the detail of our lives. I've loved that word folding ever since I took my first tentative steps in cookery, and it is precisely the right word for what I am trying to express here. It means for me, taking this somewhat alien teaching and blending it into the very texture of our lives until it becomes indistinguishable from the rest.

So what do we mean then by Buddhahood? How should we come to terms with it? The somewhat surprising fact is that it is defined quite simply, in terms of very ordinary and above all human-scale characteristics. There is nothing even vaguely superhuman about them. They are all characteristics or qualities that we could all make very good use of; an inner resource of perseverance and courage, and wisdom and compassion. What we hope to achieve, as we get better at believing in, and therefore drawing upon these qualities, is this strong and resilient and positive spirit at the core of our lives.

Of course we are all ordinary human beings, so it is in no way a static state. A place you arrive at. It is, like life itself, dynamic and constantly changing. Hence the daily-ness of the practice. But the crucial point here that needs to be emphasised is the essential, down-to-earth *humanity* of the idea. All Buddhas are ordinary human beings, immensely wise and perceptive perhaps, but still with feet of clay like the rest of us, still with their share of all the basic human qualities that we would all recognize, as an essential part of their lives, never to be got rid off. Buddhahood has got nothing to do with what might be thought of as an aspiration towards perfection, nothing to do with super-human abilities, or with transcendental powers. Just as Buddhism is about daily life, so Buddhahood can only reveal itself in the lives of ordinary people going about that ordinary everyday life.

Courage Wisdom And Compassion

Thus, courage does not mean the soldier's bravery. It is not the *absence* of fear, but the courage to overcome the fear and the negativity that we all have in our lives. Fear of so many things, fear of failure, of rejection, of isolation, of inadequacy. Winning over our own negative roadblocks is always the toughest part of any challenge. We need this everyday type of courage to confront problems as they arise, rather than brushing them under the carpet until they loom so large that they threaten to overwhelm us. It takes real courage to face up to our own greatest weaknesses.

The wisdom doesn't indicate the profound perceptions of the philosopher, but closer and deeper knowledge of ourselves, our strengths and weaknesses and the ability to perceive the patterns in our own behaviour that cause us so much suffering, so that we can set about changing them.

The compassion is not in any way *pity* for those less fortunate than ourselves but the ability to see and to comprehend the true nature of our own life and the lives of all those around us. It is much more about profound respect and understanding, for ourselves and for everyone with whom we come in contact, so that we develop a much greater level of awareness. We tend to have this powerful and instinctive need to place ourselves at the centre of our own universe, and we hear loud and clear the inner voice that shouts out our own needs and wants. We find it immensely difficult to see situations from the other person's point of view, whether it is an argument with our closest partner, or seeking to understand the nature of a Muslim fundamentalist. It is compassion that breeds the willingness to understand the other person's point of view, even when it is diametrically opposed to our own. One could certainly argue that compassion is always in short supply in today's world.

Making it Work

But those of course are just words. They mean something on the page, but that is as nothing compared with the challenge of putting them into practice. You may understand to the point of perfection the principles of tennis. You can't actually begin the game until you pick up a racket and try to hit a ball accurately.

That is pretty much the problem that I faced. I was you might say, a pretty good theoretical Buddhist. I knew a fair bit about its principles, and the more I read the more I appreciated the immense life-transforming potential of the philosophy that I had come across in what seemed to be such an accidental and inconsequential way. But that was about as far as I was prepared to go. I appreciated the understanding, but I had an immense reluctance to the process of folding it into my daily life. The reluctance was expressed in a thousand and one petty excuses. Above all perhaps I was deeply concerned about what other people might think. That may seem pretty shallow now, but it was real enough then. It had taken a long time to build up my reputation as a knowledgeable and authoritative journalist who knew a thing or two about science and technology. How could I possibly explain to all the media-sharp and cynical colleagues at work, that I had become, of all things, a Buddhist! The stereotypical image of Buddhism is that it is passive, soft-centred and mystically vague around the edges. Was I any of those things? *Could* you be a tough, inquiring television journalist and a Buddhist? None of those fears was in any way original. All of them have been faced and overcome by countless others before me. Not that that fact makes them any less daunting to each individual who faces them in turn of course.

I remember when I first took up scuba diving, and came out of the comforting surroundings of the pool and did my first deep sea dive. It was in the Eastern Mediterranean and I knew the bottom was about a 100 feet down and dark. Did I *really* want to go down there? I got into the water and fluffed around a bit on the surface, telling myself that I was sorting my gear out. Then my instructor said, "Come on. Just do it!" And we dived.

Something not dissimilar happened with Buddhism. One day Sarah, in her wisdom, persuaded me simply to stop *thinking* and to start chanting. Not a great deal, five minutes, or ten at a time. The important point was the regularity rather than the length of time. Better 10 minutes twice a day, than an hour say, once a week. At the time, it was a minor moment. Once I had started out on the journey, I carried on, and Buddhism is undoubtedly about a journey, rather than an arrival. You don't cross some huge divide, or arrive at some clearly recognisable location. It is rather, a more or less constant progression, interspersed with real moments of regression when you ask yourself, *"what on earth am I doing with all this stuff?"*

But doubts are OK I believe. Doubts are part of our essential humanity. We have doubts about everything from choosing suits to choosing partners, so it's perfectly OK to have doubts about something as big as taking Buddhism into your life. The key thing is to bring the doubts out into the open, and turn them over and have a good look at them, to understand where they come from. Only then can they be resolved.

Hang on to The Vision

But it is also important to hang onto the vision, the goal, what you are trying to achieve. You are trying to strengthen in your life the ability to see all things, that's right, *all things*, from a positive, constructive, point of view. However grey and uninspiring things might seem initially, you want to learn how you can turn them round and create value out of them, because that's the promise. But needless to say that's tough. It doesn't happen overnight. It takes time and it involves learning a new set of skills. But then so does any other skill that we seek to master. You wouldn't expect would you, to become an accomplished pianist, or a useful tennis player, unless you put in the practice?

It is in that sense that Buddhism is about daily life. We are all in the same boat. Every human life, however brilliant and scintillating and pain-free it might seem from the outside, involves fear as well as hope, despair as well as joy. The great strength of Nichiren Buddhism is that it doesn't hedge its bets. It makes a very clear and unambiguous promise. Put in the commitment it says, and you will *without fail* see the results. And the change within the individual has far wider implications. For every one of us our lives are of course, a constantly changing, constantly shifting network of relationships at every conceivable level of complexity. At the heart of Buddhism is this idea of individuals taking responsibility for their own lives. That cannot be a one-step operation, it is a continuous process, the journey along the path that we have been talking about. We summon up from somewhere the courage to set out on that path, and the Buddhist practice helps us to sustain it in our daily lives. And when we fail, as we are bound to do, it helps us to pick ourselves up and get on with it again. And again. And again, as often as it takes. But once the process has started it has very much the same effect as tossing a rock into a pond. As we change, and set about living our lives on the basis of a different set of principles, the ripples spread out in ever widening circles.

If one person changes within a close- knit group it cannot fail to have an effect upon everyone else. A more positive and optimistic approach to life, however stumbling and faltering it might be, is a powerful force for change. Buddhism teaches that it has an effect initially upon family and friends and then on colleagues and work mates. And we all recognize the truth in that. We have all had some experience of it in our daily lives. Someone with a profoundly negative or pessimistic view of life can soon drag down the spirit of an entire group. Conversely, a sunny and optimistic outlook is immensely infectious, even in difficult circumstances.

When I took up the practice, there is no doubt that the inner questioning remained persistent. Moreover I was a genuine 'closet' Buddhist, telling no one outside my innermost circle that I had taken up the practice. Despite that people at work began to notice a change in my approach. There were even wry comments like, "What are you taking these days?" I was only too well aware that I had built up a reputation for being very tough and demanding and abrasive to work with, and days on location or in the studio were often filled with a strong current of underlying tension. But I also had a reputation for producing very good results and I had come to believe for some reason that the two went hand in hand; that it was necessary to have that sort of adrenaline flowing to get the best results. I was, I now realized, profoundly wrong, and I began working really hard to change the way I approached working relationships. I became a lot easier to work with, and we produced if anything, better results. Was that change entirely due to my taking up Buddhism? It is difficult to say, but I am sure that it was the trigger that set the change within me in motion.

Buddhism argues that a fundamental change in a person's approach to life can have this enduring ripple effect, spreading out slowly, gradually, beyond family and friends, even into the local society, and beyond. It is a huge and all-embracing vision. Nichiren Buddhism teaches that a movement towards a better society, based on the principles of respect for the lives and values of others, and with peace and individual happiness as its objectives, cannot be created as a *top down* process. It has to start from the *bottom up*, with a profound change taking place within the lives of countless individuals, gradually changing the way society functions. As Daisaku Ikeda, has put it,

"There can be no lasting solution to the problems facing society that does not involve developing our own life state."

This journey towards Buddhahood then, which begins as a purely personal event, has this infinitely wider and broader vision. It is a profoundly important view of the future, a vision, one could argue, whose time has come. Rarely has there been a greater need in all societies, for these twin values that lie at the heart of Buddhism, individuals taking full responsibility for their own lives, and at the same time respecting the values and the humanity of everyone else. That is not a change that can be imposed from outside. It has to be embraced and buttressed from within.

CHAPTER FIVE

What do we Mean by Happiness?

The word happiness crops up a great deal in Buddhist discussions. You will no doubt have noticed that it has occurred on many occasions already in this account. Nichiren Buddhists will often say that the fundamental reason for their practice is nothing less than greater happiness for themselves and others. In human terms of course that is unsurprising. We do lots of things with happiness in mind, and that idea famously occupies a central position in the American Declaration of Independence;
"We hold these truths to be self evident, that all men are created equal, that they are endowed by their creator with certain unalienable Rights, that among these are Life, Liberty and the pursuit of Happiness."

In religious terms however it is rather more unusual. It is a strange fact that you have to search hard to find the word happiness in most religious liturgies. Happiness on earth that is, in the here and now, rather than happiness in some heavenly afterlife.

Buddhism, with its essential humanism and it's belief in the power of the human spirit, is strongly focused on the pursuit of happiness as the fundamental objective of human life, in the here and now. In that sense it seeks to harness what is undoubtedly one of the most powerful motivators in human life, as an engine of change, to enable us to lead fuller and richer lives. It teaches that achieving happiness, for ourselves and others, the two are always linked, is essentially what life is about. But happiness doesn't fall into our laps. Wanting it isn't achieving it. We have to learn how to achieve it. We have to take, that is, the unlikely and intractable material out of which life is fashioned, and transform it, into the stuff of happiness.

That, essentially, is why Shakyamuni left home and set out to seek an understanding of what life was really about. He had witnessed the depth of pain and suffering that was the nature of most lives on the streets of the city. What could be done about it? Was it inevitable and unavoidable, or could people come to a deeper understanding of the nature of their lives, and so create a better way to live? He knew obviously that he couldn't transform the *physical* processes of life. He had to probe more deeply into the nature and potential of the human *spirit.* The result of that quest is the body of teachings that we call Buddhism.

But what do we mean therefore by *happiness*? It is undoubtedly an immensely slippery and elusive state to define, since it is by its very nature so subjective.

What is clear is that, rather like the taste of the strawberry, however difficult it may be to define, we know it when we experience it. Equally we are strongly aware of its absence. If we look back in our own lives for example it seems that it is defined most readily by reference to particular experiences. We tend to think of happy times or moments in our life, periods that came and went, episodes, rather than a "state of happiness." When we lived in a particular place perhaps, or when we were on holiday somewhere; when we were in a sports team at school, or when we mastered a particular skill, or when we first went to work, or fell in love. For most of us the actual experience of happiness is transient and fleeting in this way. Short bursts of this experience called happiness, interspersed with perhaps longer periods when it wasn't there, or at least not strongly enough to have planted a warm, glowing feeling in our memory.

Why not we might ask? Because an answer to such a question might clearly give us an oblique insight into what constitutes this elusive experience that we call happiness. Had it just faded and gone away? Or was it overlaid by the experiences of *non-happiness*, if I may call it that, which caused greater or lesser bouts of anxiety? Coping with a broken relationship for example, or a boring and unsatisfying job from which there seemed to be no escape, nagging financial worries, or a persistent lack of self worth eating away at one's confidence. The list of possible dissatisfactions of course is endless, we all have our own private agonies that we chew over.

But the point I am making is that in general, our sense of happiness seems very much to be tied to *external* events. This happens, we like it and feel happy. That happens, we don't like it and we feel unhappy. A bit like a cork in a swell, bobbing up and down with every wave that passes. And if we look at key social indicators on which there is so much research these days, the incidence of broken families and relationships for example, or drug taking or prescriptions for anti-depressants like Vallium and Prozac, there is plenty of evidence to suggest that the sorts of things that trigger the periods of non- happiness, are, if anything, increasing. It would seem that the *potential* for an underlying, ever-present, restless dissatisfaction with our lives is greater than it has ever been.

Why might that be, and where might we turn for an explanation?

Well, as it happens these days, even in a field as elusive as happiness, we can turn at least in some measure to science. Over the past few years there has been a huge amount of social and psychological research seeking to define what makes people feel good about themselves and their life state. Much of it, as you might expect has taken place in America, where the pursuit of happiness is after all, a central plank in the constitution!

For most of its history psychology has concerned itself with what assails and disables the human mind. Psychologists have spent many decades focusing largely on the causes of depression and anxiety, and seeking to move people from a negative or ailing state to a neutral normal. More recently they have come to believe that more value is to be created from an understanding of what kinds of factors contribute to a deep-seated sense of well being. Indeed it has blossomed in the past decade or so, into a new and valuable academic field in its own right, the study of Positive Psychology.

As psychologist Professor Martin Seligman from the University of Pennsylvania, one of the prime architects of the new direction, has paraphrased it:

"It wasn't enough for us to nullify disabling conditions and get to zero. We needed to ask what are the enabling conditions

that make human beings flourish? How do we get from zero to plus five?"*

That having been said, the social scientists still find it very difficult indeed to define precisely what happiness *is*, as indeed one might expect, since it can only be defined in terms of personal experience. But if we look at some of the findings that have emerged in recent years, from the research carried out in this field, on what sorts of experiences generate a profound sense of well being, it is extraordinary how closely they mirror so many of the teachings that are embodied in Nichiren's countless letters to his followers.

Altruism for example, somewhat unexpectedly comes very high on the list, concerning oneself with the needs and welfare of others rather than focusing on one's own current problems. Evolutionary biologists still have very great difficulty in fathoming out the evolutionary value of altruism, but here it is, revealed as a primary source of human happiness. The remarkable power of gratitude is a recurrent theme, unlocking not just a sense of well being in both the giver and the receiver, but better health and more energy. Professor Seligman for example describes how simply going out of one's way to express gratitude to someone can have a beneficial effect on the giver's sense of well being even *a month* after it has taken place.

In his book *Authentic Happiness* Seligman is one of many who places great emphasis on what he calls "engagement," or the depth of involvement with the lives of those around us, family, friends and work colleagues; having an awareness and understanding of our wider humanity and our relationship to others. He also stresses the need for a strong sense of purpose, having some goal or direction that is bigger and wider than the simple daily progression of our lives.

But what kind of explanation have the psychologists come up with to account for this restless modern dissatisfaction or malaise outlined earlier. Dr Edward Diener, from the University of Illinois, one of the prime movers in the field of Positive Psychology, argues that it may be seen as the *downside* of today's vastly greater affluence.

The Material Dead End

It is seen to arise from the fact that so much more is available, that there is so much more out there to be hungered after, which represents a powerful external cause of inner discontent. We are constantly being called upon to measure who we are, and what we have, against role models who are presented as being, in various ways, highly successful, better off, and therefore, by implication, *happier.* It's a truism to say that happiness is very widely measured these days in terms of material display, what we have. The new car, the big house, the fashionable clothes, and so on. That is of course, the way modern marketing and advertising work, playing with great skill on the natural human tendency to compare ourselves with others, and to see thereby much more clearly what we haven't got, as opposed to what we have. Nichiren even touched upon something very similar in one of his letters all those years ago;

"For example, a poor man cannot earn a penny just by counting his neighbours wealth, even if he does so night and day."*

In that sense, modern lifestyle marketing is an undeniably disturbing influence in our environment, constantly throwing up before our eyes, images of people who have bigger, better, more elegant, more beautiful, more powerful…. cars, clothes, houses, furniture, bodies, or whatever. The range of material possessions has never been greater, and with the global reach of modern film and television, the circle of comparison into which we are drawn has widened to take in the entire world. The consequent potential for what one might call "induced" dissatisfaction with our lot is all the greater, vast indeed. And it is not simply a matter of envy. It is both deeper and wider than that. If we can't achieve these sorts of symbols of success, we tell ourselves, then what's wrong with us? Clearly we are in some measure a failure, we just don't have what it takes to succeed in life. And since success means happiness in this equation, we just don't have what it takes to be truly happy.

Positive Psychology has even coined a name to describe this condition. Its called "reference anxiety."

That having been said, it is important to emphasise that Nichiren Buddhism is not about *giving up* material possessions. It embraces both the material and the spiritual aspects of life, since both are clearly important to us. The key, it argues, to a profound sense of well being is recognizing that we need to establish some kind of balance. To be human is to want to have things. It's part of our nature. Our direct prehistoric ancestors for example, may be said to have introduced the consumer society 30-40,000 years ago, in the shape of shell necklaces and decorated beads, and beautifully hand carved, personalised hunting weapons called spear-throwers. Decoration didn't make them work any better. They just looked more pleasing, so that they were more desirable. What's more, they traded them all over Europe. It hasn't stopped since then. Wanting things is undoubtedly one of the main driving forces of life. And basic desires for things like a good job and material comforts and so on, are deeply woven into our humanity, and should in no way be set aside, or seen as somehow less worthy.

People who take up this practice are positively encouraged to chant for whatever it is they believe they feel they need in their lives, and that might certainly include material benefits, from a better income and financial security, to a better house for example, and everything in between. The argument being that the act of chanting will inevitably bring forth the wisdom and the compassion to put those desires into a proper, broader, whole-life context.

What it does say however, is that while acquiring new things may well be an extremely pleasurable experience, it is unlikely to be the basis for the solid, lasting, resilient happiness that we all seek. The pleasure in new possessions, soon wears off, and the only way to re-ignite that sort of pleasure is to get going again, into another bout of retail therapy, to buy or acquire more stuff. We've all been some way down that road. All we need, we persuade ourselves, is that "something else," in the showroom window, and then well be more or less content. And then something else pops into our vision, and on… and on.

Since it lies at the root of a great deal of pain and suffering, Buddhism gives this itch to acquire, a name. It's called the life state of Hunger, a state of almost permanent, restless dissatisfaction, in which we are utterly convinced that happiness lies in having something or experiencing something, that at this precise moment, is just out of our reach. That particular delusion is not limited of course to material things, it reaches out into all the fields of human activity, from the desire for partners and children, to wealth and fame, and on to permanent youth and beauty. It is not un- common for people in this state of hunger to fix their gaze on one thing after another in their environment, in the conviction, each time, that *it* will satisfy their yearning, and bring them the happiness that just eludes them. Hunger of this kind is the cause of a great deal of deep and enduring unhappiness.

Buddhism argues therefore, that although desires are natu- ral and essential to life and to be encouraged, it is a profoundly unhappy-making delusion to believe that lasting happiness can be acquired in this way, externally as it were, along with some possession or other; that you can somehow *buy* your way into it.

The Problem-Free Existence

The underlying desire that most of us share for a problem- free existence, is, if you like, a special category of that delu- sion. It may seem to be something completely different, but in fact it shares many of the same characteristics.

None of us wants problems. Ever. We know in our bones that problems and crises, difficulties and challenges of one kind or another, are an inescapable part of our existence. But for some reason, deep within the human psyche, we cling on to the strongly held belief, or the hope perhaps, that problems, and the suffering they bring are the *exception* rather than the rule. The net result is that happiness, in a sense, comes to be defined as the *absence* of problems. And since the reality of course is that problems, challenges, difficulties of one kind or another continue to come pretty much all the time, in one area of our life or another, the happiness we seek continues to elude us.

Given this view of life, it is very often the case that in our deep desire to avoid problems and the suffering we associate with them, we adopt all kinds of ruses to deflect them. We try to ignore them, or run away from them, in the hope that they will somehow evaporate. The reality of course, as we all know to our costs, is that problems ignored can very often become problems magnified. What was once readily soluble if only we had had the courage to face up to it, often becomes something so big that it overwhelms us.

We are accustomed for example, to pointing outside ourselves to others, or to other circumstances in our environment, anything so long as it is not ourselves, as the source of our current predicament or difficulties. If there are difficulties within a relationship, for example, it is because the *other* party to the arrangement has to change something about themselves, or has some particularly awkward or annoying habit. If there's friction with the boss at work it's likely to be because of his or her totally unreasonable or unfair behaviour. Indeed a common approach to dealing with problems like this, is to ignore them, because we see them as someone else's fault. Either we pretend that they're not there, or we refuse to confront them, sweep them under the carpet.

That is particularly true in relationships where there might be an underlying difference of view. One party feels it very strongly, the other party just brushes it aside, hoping it will go away. And what starts out perhaps as quite a small issue between loving partners, builds up enough pressure to blow the relationship apart.

At the other end of the spectrum there is the sense of hopelessness that many people experience, not necessarily because of the scale, or the number of problems, but because of the sense of powerlessness or impotence that they create.

The basic premise of Buddhism is that everything, but everything, begins with the self. If there's friction or difficulty or frustration coming from various quarters in our life, then the place to look for the cause is *within our own life.* However hard that may be to accept. It is the real meaning of taking responsibility for your life. What is it about *our* thoughts or words or actions that is giving rise to the trouble. That is, admittedly, an uncomfortable-making premise. It's hard to swallow. But the huge upside of that premise is that if the cause comes from within, so too can the solution. It lies within our grasp. Not, *"If only he or she would change…"* but *"What action can I take, what things about myself can I change to resolve the problem?"*

Happiness is not in Someone Else's Gift

The greatness of Nichiren Buddhism as a philosophy lies in its immense practicality. It sets out to explain how life works, and how it can be lived happily, and creatively, *as it really is,* not how we might wish it to be. Shakyamuni Buddha wasn't a theoretician, he spent all his teaching life in and among people, answering their questions, offering them new ways of thinking about their situation. Nichiren Daishonin came out of the same mould. He didn't sit in solitary meditation in some monastery. He spent all his time in the thick of life, grappling with the problems of ordinary people, at a time when the country was in constant turmoil.

The result, as so many thousands of people have learned, is that both Shakyamuni and Nichiren deliver a teaching that is at once immensely practical, and immensely liberating.

Namely, that there is absolutely nothing to be gained from either railing at problems, as they continue to occur in our lives, or to base our hopes for happiness on some longed-for, problem-free future. The key, Nichiren, writes, is to get on with things,

"Though worldly troubles may arise, never let them disturb you. No one can avoid problems, not even sages or worthies.'

Our happiness, that is, is not in someone else's gift. The kind of durable, underlying happiness that provides a basis for one's life, and that is not dependant on external events, can only come from one place. It has to come from within.

It is this change of response within ourselves, that alone determines the extent to which we can win or lose in creating a happy life. When we are weak, our problems seem to loom over us and become insurmountable, an Everest to be climbed. When our spirit is strong, they shrink in size, and become no more than a challenge that we know we can set out to overcome.

Moreover, this perception transforms the whole nature of the equation. The challenge now becomes not so much how to cope with the problem, but how to make ourselves *stronger,* how to build up this inner resolve so that we are not bowled over when the problem comes at us. That change is the very heart of the matter, and one of the central promises, of the practice of Nichiren Buddhism, is that it steadily builds up our inner confidence, and sense of self worth.

The Only Spiritual Gym in Town

The extraordinary paradox that lies at the very heart of this practice is, that it is not enough just to see problems and difficulties as an *inevitable* factor in our lives. We need to learn to see them as *essential* to our growth and happiness. Our common response is likely to be, "Problems, who needs them?" But it doesn't take very much reflection to see the life-transforming power of the idea, that problems and difficulties, pain and grief, can in fact be the stimulus for our greatest growth.

The ever-present pull of gravity on Earth for example, weighing down upon us, has forced our body to grow and evolve a physique so strong and so muscular that we can not only walk upright, but we can run and jump and leap over obstacles, and not even be aware of the burden.

Similarly, Nichiren writes,

"Only by defeating a powerful enemy can one prove one's real strength."*

Thus the essential Buddhist proposition is that problems and difficulties provide the means, the opportunity if you like, for our spiritual work out. And if you think about it for a moment, they represent the *only* spiritual gym in town; the essential challenge without which we simply cannot develop the spiritual muscle we need to live a full and happy life. There is no other.

Nobody is saying that that is an easy lesson to learn or to apply, but the fact is, we all have some experience of how it works.

When we overcome problems, we *do* feel a huge sense of personal achievement. We get a job we didn't expect to get, or we overcome a tough illness, or we manage to help a friend overcome a bout of anxiety over some really challenging problem in their life, and the victory gives us a powerful sense of elation. And the bigger the problem overcome, the greater the sense of elation. For a while we feel strengthened and uplifted, and we sense a much greater confidence in our ability to handle life, not just in that particular set of circumstances, but right across the range of our experience and activity. That is a key point. The effect is as broad and as far reaching as that. From that increased confidence comes the greatly increased sense of well being.

Basically all that Buddhism is encouraging us to do is to hang on to that idea, to be aware of it, and to build on and reinforce it with the energy or the inner confidence that comes from the daily practice. Thus instead of it being a fleeting and occasional experience, it can become a daily one.

That is the shift in attitude that we are seeking. The problems remain the same, but our sense of being able to overcome them has changed profoundly. Problems that we feel confident that we can overcome change in character. They are no longer so threatening or anxiety-creating. In fact we consciously change the words we use to describe them. We call them *challenges*, and the change is immensely significant. Problems are negative and 'downcasting,' challenges are stimulating and uplifting.

It is important to emphasise that we are not talking about stoicism, about simply *putting up* with difficulties, or about trying to be broad shouldered in bearing a burden. It is about *transforming* those inevitable difficulties into the source of a more consistent sense of well being, for ourselves and those around us.

Thus a teaching that might at first seem strange, not to say unreal, is in fact immensely liberating. Nichiren Buddhists often describe this approach to problems with the phrase "turning poison into medicine." That is to say, taking a difficult, even impossible situation, and not simply enduring it, but turning it around completely, to create value and fulfilment out of crisis.

Knowing Where to Look

I have to admit that I found it extremely difficult in those early days, to talk about Buddhism and happiness in the beautifully bold and confident way that many other Buddhists around me did, just as I found it difficult to talk about the idea of attaining Buddhahood. But I found the idea that lies right at the heart of this Buddhist practice immensely powerful and moving. Namely that whether we realize it or not, whether we believe it or not, whether we understand it or not, we have within ourselves the power to *choose* happiness in this life, and that we can actually learn how to achieve that goal. That is unquestionably a life-changing concept. Happiness does not mean absence of problems or challenges. But it does mean a strong, enduring sense of the *value* of our lives from moment to moment, and the value of the lives of every other human being.

That is easy to say. It is extremely difficult to achieve. Few of us I think really know how to value the quality of our lives from moment to moment, despite the fact that we can readily appreciate just how valuable a quality it might be. It is something we have to learn how to acquire. And there is basically only one way to do it, and that is, working at it, reminding ourselves of it every single day. Why not? It is that valuable! It's a bit like piano practice, it's little by little. You only get to play Mozart if you work at it every day.

Thus, a key factor in this wholly natural quest for happiness is learning where to look. Buddhism teaches us, paradoxically, that if we believe that our happiness in this life is dependant on the absence of problems and difficulties, then that is a strategy doomed to failure, since there is no such place. If, on the other hand we seek a strong, durable, sense of well being at the core of our lives, that can *only* be found in the very midst of the problems life throws at us, essentially by growing the courage and the wisdom to challenge and to overcome them.

That may sound on the face of it to be a rather uncomfortable and unlikely route to the happiness that we are all seeking. But, it is, when you think about it, both immensely clear-eyed, and practical. Above all, it's built to last, since it is constructed out of the real circumstances of our lives. And it comes from within, so it is not dependent upon the ever-changing circumstances of human life. We all love the elation and the surge of joy that comes from some sudden success or a desire fulfilled. Life would be very much the poorer without it. We all like the idea of the buzz associated with wealth or status. But above all we want the enduring, indestructible sense of well being that Nichiren Buddhism describes as absolute, rather than relative.

So, we have at least part of the answer to that opening question. It turns out that for Buddhism, happiness certainly does not mean the temporary rapture that comes in response to some exciting external event. It is not about acquisition. It is not fundamentally dependant upon someone else. It does mean, on the other hand, getting closer to our own Buddha nature.

The Story of Sally

"I had been practicing Nichiren Buddhism for about five years. I loved the practice and it brought immense joy and sense of stability into my life. But there was a deep and unfulfilled need at the heart of my life.

More than anything in my life I wanted to be a mother. I had always wanted children but now the desire was overwhelming. It was the first thought that came into my head every morning, and often the last thing I thought about at night. I was only recently married, and my husband John and I had talked about this a great deal before we got married, so I knew that it was going to be immensely difficult, if not impossible. John had had a vasectomy some years earlier. He went into hospital before we got married to reverse the operation, but it was only partially successful. A problem that we hadn't anticipated was the medical advice we received. As I understood it, the antibodies triggered by the original vasectomy operation were killing, or severely weakening any sperm that were produced.

My hopes of finding some way out of this cul de sac took a nose dive. But I desperately wanted us to have our *own* child, made up of me and John. Once again I couldn't think my way through this terrible dilemma, and I decided that the only recourse I had was to test the practice to the very limit. I remember thinking, *"What is the point of this practice, if it cannot help me* through the most important challenge of my life. *What is the point?"* I decided that whatever happened, I would chant two hours a day, until I was holding *our* baby in my arms. I cannot begin to explain what courage it took to do that.

I don't know in fact where the courage came from.

When I made that commitment I was almost afraid that I had made it. It seemed that I had created a mountain for myself, and now I had to struggle up it. I couldn't see how I was going to do it. I set the alarm on day one for 6 am and just started. In retrospect it was a terrible struggle. I cried a great deal in front of the Gohonzon * until my eyes were red. My chanting wasn't brave and strong. Often I was just creeping along with this little thin voice coming out. I also knew that we needed to take some action, so we began the rounds of the fertility clinics.

My spirits were low, and the response was always the same. The chance of our having our own baby was given as less than 1%. That is to say, impossible. I still have that letter, it had such a powerful effect on me. I was advised to think of adoption, or having donor sperm.

I never missed a single day, but nothing changed. Nothing. The challenge didn't get any less. By now John was really concerned about how I was tackling this, and he strongly advised me to accept donor sperm. He promised to love the baby that resulted with all his strength. But I knew now that I couldn't possibly go down that route until I had tested out every possible opportunity to have our baby. I simply could-n't give up.

---

* Footnote. The scroll that Nichiren Buddhists receive when they take up the practice. See detailed explanation in Chapter 16

I determined that I would continue the two hours chanting, however difficult it was, and that I needed somehow to extend the action that was taking. Out of the blue the opportunity came up to go on a Buddhist study course in Japan. I couldn't really afford it, but I decided that somehow I had to go.

The course was inspirational and deeply moving. I met so many Japanese people who had been practising for many years and who were welcoming beyond measure. And I remember so clearly their constant guidance,"Whatever you do, just don't give up the practice."

When I came back the situation hadn't really changed, but I had a much stronger determination, and I knew now without any qualification, that I would not relinquish my two hours chanting a day, until I had my baby in my arms. We decided first of all that we needed to test out the medical advice again to ensure that we had explored every loophole. The advice turned out to be the same, and John was by now imploring me to take the simpler donor sperm route. But then, one day, in the corner of yet another Harley Street waiting room, tucked away behind some papers at the edge of a notice board, I saw a small calling card offering a special IVF technique. I grabbed at this tiny window of opportunity. There was one huge drawback. It was in Brussels. John did all he could to dissuade me, because he was fearful of the effects on me of yet another wild goose chase. But by now I was very strong. And so our visits to Brussels began.

They weren't easy. Every kind of obstacle seemed to plant itself in our path. We misplaced tickets inexplicably. We forgot time differences and arrived an hour late for appointments. Flights were overbooked and we were bumped off them. But I remembered so strongly the guidance I had received, that when you are changing your life profoundly then undoubtedly problems will arise, and you have to summon up all the perseverance you possess to press on.

The advice in Brussels was subtly different. The chances of having *our* baby was still less than 1%, for as long as John was producing immotile sperm. But if he could produce even a minute sample of sperm that were in any way motile, then it would be possible to create embryos for implanting, and they saw no reason medically why that should not be possible. It really depended on our willingness to persevere. I have also kept that letter, the consultant's report containing that diagnosis.

It now became a question of our joint courage. By now my two hours a day was an inseparable part of my life. Not easy, but nothing could have made me give up. John agreed to start to chant for the possibility of producing motile sperm.

In the space of about a year I had changed my life. I had got married, and travelled from despair about my baby, to a position of real hope. John had travelled from outright opposition, to being immensely supportive of the practice. Some weeks later we travelled to Brussels for the crucial event. Either they would be able to produce embryos on this occasion, or this window too would be closed to us. On the day he was due to produce a sample John drove to the clinic and sat outside and chanted for an hour before he went in. When they tested the sample the doctors could scarcely believe what they saw. There were more than enough motile sperm. Everything was now possible.

Thirty six hours later we received the phone call at the hotel saying that they had been able to create a batch of healthy embryos. I couldn't sleep that night, and I could scarcely chant the next morning I was so nervous.

The difficulties hadn't quite gone away. The next morning, while I was in the operating theatre and John was waiting outside, our bag was stolen from the consultant's office, with all our tickets and passports and money and cards. We were destitute in Brussels. But it was as nothing, in relation to the huge victory that we had achieved against all odds, and the fierce elation in my heart. I can't even remember how we got over those difficulties, they seemed so trivial.

I continued to chant for two hours a day. And waited. My pregnancy was perhaps the happiest time of my life. Nine months later, well eight months in fact, because he couldn't wait to arrive, my beautiful son, *our* son, was born.

I cannot think of an area of my life that has not been changed by the courage and the resolution that have been developed through my practice."

CHAPTER SIX

States of Mind

Buddhism seeks to explain the reality of daily life. It does not present in any way a sort of utopian ideal, or an abstract vision of what might be. It is absolutely real, so real that you can grab hold of it. It is a rich and detailed analysis of the nature of human life, built up on the basis of the observations and perceptions, as well as the inspiration, of some quite exceptionally gifted and enlightened people, whom we happen to call Buddhas. It is not scientific, but there are many comparisons to be made with scientific observation. It is no accident that modern psychology for example, is deeply interested in many of the conclusions that Buddhism has arrived at, about the essential nature of human life. As the late philosopher and historian Arnold Toynbee has written, *"The Buddhist analysis of the dynamics of life is more detailed and subtle than any modern Western analysis I know of."*

The concept of the ten worlds or the ten states of life is just such an analysis of the dynamics of human life. Its purpose is to describe for us in a way that is systematic, and therefore practical and useful, something that we all experience, but which we take so much for granted, as a normal part of our lives, that we rarely give it a moments thought. That something, is the extraordinary, moment- to- moment change-ability in our state of mind, as we go about our daily lives.

We all know that our life state, or how we feel changes constantly throughout the day, triggered by the constant flux of thoughts within, and the stream of events we encounter without. Our mind is like quicksilver, it is so rapid in its response to every stimulus. And everything that we sense or that we experience calls forth a response. Every hour is different, every minute, at times every second even, so swift is the ability of the mind to respond to what is going on in and around us.

Since Buddhism is entirely about the ordinary daily lives of ordinary human beings, it has to cope with this feature of our lives, and the concept of the ten worlds is the result. It goes without saying that they are not objective places, these worlds, they are of course purely subjective states, inside our head, states of mind.

Although it might seem when one first encounters the concept, to be somewhat implausible to say the least, to reduce the vast range of our constantly shifting responses to just 10 states. But stay your judgement till you have explored the idea a little further. It is worth bearing in mind that this is a structure that has undoubtedly stood the test of time. More-over, it does pass the all- important test of *practicality*. If there were 50, or 100 life states for example, it would become wholly unwieldy and impractical as a way of thinking about our lives.

That is a crucial point. The ten worlds, as a fundamental prin-ciple of Buddhism, is not intended for the bookshelves, or for the psychiatrists couch. It is of value only to the extent that it is *useful* in our daily lives. It provides us in a sense with a sort of road map, an A-Z of our inner life state. This is where you are, where do you want to be? With this structure we are offered a thoughtful and detailed and above all, *objective* guide to help us interpret where we are in our *subjective* or emotional life, so that we can see it more clearly and do something about it. If, as Buddhism teaches, both suffering and happiness come not from the external factors in our lives, but from deep within, then knowing more clearly where we are, as opposed to where we would like to be, is a crucial piece of information. Indeed one might say, where else are we going to get that information? And this is not superficial stuff. The life states we are in from moment to moment affect *everything* in our life, how we feel, how we think, how we act, even how we look, not to mention how our environment responds to us.

With a moment's reflection we can all recognize the truth in that. When we are in the state of anger for example, it is instantly signalled by the flushed face, and the stiffening in the facial muscles, and the raised pitch of the voice. That set of indicators is likely to trigger an immediate tension in the environment. Everybody responds to it with their own heightened tension and increased attention to what's going on. If somebody happens to prick the tension with a joke or a laugh, in an instant it's gone, the muscles in the face relax, the voice is lowered again, the eyes lose their glitter, the tension in the room dissipates. It's all there, how we feel in those contrasting moments, how we think, act, and look, and how our environment responds.

Another important point to emphasise is that these ten states are not in any way represented as a sort of subjective or emotional *ladder,* on which we might move up or down, in any progressive way. These ten life states represent rather the entire universe of our mind, and we move from any part of that universe to any other part in a trice, depending on what is taking place within our minds and without, from moment to moment.

There is however a basic problem in putting this idea across. The movement of our mind is so dazzlingly swift, and words by comparison are so slow and cumbersome, that any attempt to describe these kaleidoscopic changes in our subjective or emotional life, *in words*, inevitably appears somewhat laboured and unreal. It feels, and no doubt reads, a bit like walking in wet concrete, everything is slowed down and slightly caricatured.

Bearing that caution in mind let's look briefly at all ten subjective life states.

Hell

Hell is a state of the deepest suffering or depression, often characterised by a feeling of helplessness; we feel cannot escape the pain we are in, we just have to endure it. There are many gradations of course, from the somewhat superficial hell of having a really bad day at the office when everything goes against you and just nothing goes right, to the despair and panic at being made redundant, and not knowing where you're going to find another job, to the deep, deep grief at the loss of a child or a partner, when you cannot believe that the darkness will ever lift. We feel grey within, and everything seems dull and grey without.

We all recognize this state as being real, part of all our lives. The examples are as many and varied as there are people to experience them. When we have been in Hell state the memory of it remains with us for a long time, sometimes for ever.

We are told that all these life states have both a positive and a negative dimension, but can there possibly be a positive dimension to Hell? Buddhism argues that there is. The deep suffering can be the greatest possible stimulus to action. We feel compelled to summon up from somewhere the life force to enable us to climb out of the hole that our life has fallen into. It is also a great teacher, in the sense that having been there ourselves, we are immensely more capable of understanding and feeling compassion for, and finding the right way to support, others who are in Hell state now, as Joanna's story makes clear (see page 124).

Hunger

We've already touched on hunger briefly, but to fill the picture out a little, the world of Hunger is essentially a state of more or less permanent dissatisfaction with where your life is now, because your wants or your desires have got out of control. It's the out of control bit that is the problem. Desires are of course fundamental to our human nature, essential to life in so many ways. They motivate us towards satisfying our basic needs for food and warmth and love and friendship, and move us on to satisfy the needs for status and recognition and reward and pleasure. Once again there are many gradations of this life state, from a constant nagging, but bearable, itch to have some new thing or experience, to the stage where the hunger has, in a sense become an end in itself, so that it can never be satisfied. We end up chasing one desire after another, and yet experiencing no real sense of fulfilment or satisfaction. As soon as the desire has been achieved, the hunger seeks out yet another object to be possessed. A more common term for it I suppose might be good old fashioned greed. Since whatever we have is not enough we end up trapped in a world of frustrated yearning, another kind of hell. We are in the grip of a genuine addiction, and like most addictions, it is associated with a great deal of suffering not only for oneself, but for all those around us.

What about the positive dimension of Hunger? It lies in the fact that there is a huge amount of drive and energy locked up in the hunger state. If that energy can be re-directed or re-channelled, away from satisfying our selfish ends towards, meeting the needs of others who may be severely deprived in various ways, then such hunger can move mountains and achieve great good.

Animality

As the title itself suggests, animality defines a life state in which one is driven pretty much by instinct, with little or no moderation from reason or from moral consid-erations. So this is a state in which the strong, or those in the know, would take advantage of the weak or those who are unaware, in order to satisfy their own ends, regardless of the rights or the morality of the situation.

This state is often described as one governed by the law of the jungle, but these days we might more readily talk of mindless hooliganism, and reckless anti-social behaviour, in which the perpetrators take no account of the suffering or the anxiety inflicted on the people around them. One could argue perhaps that we are being a little hard on the animals when we define this sort of semi-psychopathic human behaviour in relation to them. But the point is clear enough, fundamental to this life state is an absence of humanity. It is also charac-terised by an absence of wisdom or lack of judgement. So that in a state of animality we don't care whether our behaviour is appropriate or not. We just go ahead and do whatever we want, regardless of other people's feelings or needs. Similarly we pay scant attention to things like rules and regulations that are designed to keep things running smoothly in our crowded urban environments.

These three states are known in Buddhism as the three evil paths, not so much because they are associated with evil in the conventional sense, but because they are the root cause of a great deal of suffering. They can tear lives apart or render them unbearable. People in these life states tend to rotate through them in swift succession, one after the other, driven by their hunger for one thing or another, not really aware of the effect on other people, creating a great deal of pain and suffering, and little of value, in their own lives and the lives of people close to them. In that sense they are desperate life states, and one of the great virtues that stems from knowledge of the ten worlds is that it can act like a clarion call. It can make you starkly aware of the reality of your situation and thus act as a powerful stimulus to lift you out of it. Few people would want to continue to dwell in hell state or hunger or animality, once they realize where they are.

Anger

Anger is a state in which one's life is dominated not simply by the external manifestations of anger, the shouting and the threats and the storms of temper, but by the constant over- weaning demands of one's ego. At its heart is the sense of superiority over others, with all the distortions of perspective that entails. So there will be the sudden outbursts of blazing anger that may seem to come from nowhere, often surprising the owner of the anger as much as the hapless victim. But there will also be lots of other destructive behaviour such as rampant intolerance, and cynicism and sarcasm, lack of gratitude and constant criticism of other people's work. People in Anger state often find it just as difficult to live with themselves, as other people find it to be with them, because they seem to have no real control over the source of the anger. The flaring temper and the disabling cynicism and backbiting just seem to well up from nowhere.

It goes without saying that anger of this sort can be immensely destructive of personal relationships. At the wider level of society, anger in the sense of superiority of self, clearly lies at the root of a whole range of widespread injustices, from racism and religious intolerance, to the oppression of women and minority groups.

But there is a positive side to Anger, because it is also a great achiever. It can be a powerful, highly energised driver towards change, in the fight against apathy for example, or when it takes on causes that challenge the dignity of the individual.

Once again the key to overcoming the destructive side of anger has to come from self -awareness. It can't just be switched off or re-directed from *outside.* Each individual has to struggle to change his or her life from within.

Humanity

Humanity is a life state in which we are in a sense calm and in control of ourselves, more or less at peace with our lot. So it is fundamentally a neutral state where nothing has excited or upset, or aroused a passionate response. It is sometimes called a state of rest because it is at least partly about recharging one's batteries. It is marked therefore by lots of positive qualities such as reasonableness and sound judgement and consideration for others and the ability to see clearly between truth and falsehood. When you are in this state it means that you are actively seeking to achieve compromise rather than conflict, or putting the best gloss on circumstances rather than being hyper-critical. It might be the moment of apology after flying off the handle over something, or perhaps working really hard not to lose your temper when someone is being totally unreasonable.

The negative aspect of this life state might be a certain amount of apathy, revealed in long term acceptance of an unsatisfactory status quo, or an unwillingness to make an effort.

Rapture or Heaven

We have already discussed the life state of rapture to some extent in the discussion of happiness. Rapture represents what is described in Buddhism as *relative* happiness. As it's name suggests, it is the wonderful up-welling of joy and exhilaration that we experience when we achieve something that we desire strongly. It brings with it the sense of personal fulfilment and the zest for life and the outburst of energy that comes with winning something we have really set our heart on, or setting off on holiday perhaps, or falling in love. Indeed the modern ideal of romantic love is perhaps the most accurate metaphor for what we mean by rapture. It has been said that in our modern culture, the desire for romantic love has become so strong that it has virtually replaced religion as a main source of spiritual fulfilment. But however wonderful and exhilarating it may be, however much it enriches our life, the reality is that by its very nature, rapture is short lived, a sudden peak of joy in the normal curve of our lives.

Although many people today are inclined to equate this essentially unstable and transient state with the highest possible state of life, and yearn for some way of making it permanent in their lives, Buddhism teaches that the idea of permanent rapture is simply unreal. It only takes the passage of time or even a slight change of circumstances for that peak of exhilaration or joy to pass, to be replaced by another life state. It is by definition transient; the yearning for it to stay and be there forever, a permanent part of our lives, is a delusion that can only lead to suffering.

These six worlds from Hell to Rapture, describe the reality of life for most of us, and one of the key insights that Nichiren Buddhism offers, is that we experience them very much in response to changes in our *external* circumstances. They are very closely interlinked, and we can slip very easily from one to another. And as we fluctuate between these states we are pretty much at the mercy of our environment, now up, now down, now left now right. Clearly that represents an immensely vulnerable situation to be in. The clear implication is that our life state, and in a sense therefore, our *identity*, from moment to moment, how we think and feel and behave and look, is dependent to a considerable extent, upon what comes to us from without. Happy when things seem to be going well. Unhappy when they don't. It leaves us somewhat like a rudderless boat, blown this way and that by whatever winds that blow, bounced up and down by whatever waves that strike us. Not a situation that is likely to produce anything resembling enduring happiness. Not the best way to live.

The remaining four life states are very different. They are called the Four Noble Paths: Learning, Realization, Bodhisattva and Buddhahood. They could be described as representing the great potential in human life, not simply responding to movements in our environment in a reactionary or an opportunistic way, but taking control of our lives to make the very most of them. They are all marked by the very considerable *effort* that is required from us to achieve them.

The sixth and seventh life states, **LEARNING** and **REALIZATION** are often taken together because they are closely related. Both are concerned with a strong desire for self-improvement, although via different routes. Learning essentially describes the process of study, putting ourselves in the position where we can take on board the knowledge and the insights of others and apply them to our own life. So it might be equated to some extent with our attitude towards learning or the desire to discuss, or the ability to absorb knowledge.

Realization, on the other hand, describes the process of inner reflection or consideration that enables us to work on the knowledge that we have acquired, or the experiences we have been through, to achieve a different level of understanding of life. In this sense it might be equated with our wisdom or our intuition.

Those who work professionally, so to speak, in the fields of learning and realisation, such as teachers and doctors and scientists and writers are clearly likely to spend rather more time in these life states than most of us, but they apply equally to any kind of learning or reflection that we might be involved in. Learning a new trade or skill for example to get a better job, exercising a hobby or a pastime, appreciating an art exhibition, taking part in a discussion group to share experiences.

These life states also have their negative as well as their positive aspects however. Knowledge can bring with it a sense of superiority for example, over those who don't have it, doctors for patients, professors for students, scientists for the ignorance of the general public.

Up till now all these life states have been given ordinary names, using words like hell and hunger and anger that are in common currency. The next two are defined by names that we would never use in any other context. Bodhisattva and Buddhahood are not just relatively unfamiliar, they are essentially *technical* terms coming from Buddhist literature. The important thing is to get behind the names themselves so that we can relate them to our everyday behaviour.

Bodhisattva

The hallmark of the life state of Bodhisattva is caring for others, being concerned about their welfare or their safety or their general well being. Spending time with an older person perhaps, giving time to a charity, giving of oneself in all sorts of ways to support and improve the lives of others. It is, you will remember, one of the primary qualities that modern psychological research suggests is fundamental to happiness in this life.

At its heart is the desire, not simply to help other people, but fundamentally to alleviate the cause of their pain or suffering, and to replace it with a greater sense of well being.

One of the most immediate paths out of the life states such as Hell and Hunger and Anger is indeed, to find some way, however small, to contribute to the lives of others.

The prime example of this degree of compassion for others is perhaps the mother, or the parent, whose concern for the child is unconditional. Nothing is too much. Mothers as we know can be totally bound up with the child's health and growth and happiness. Other obvious examples would be the nurse and the doctor and the social worker. Or the aid workers, prepared to place themselves in difficult and even dangerous circumstances in developing countries for example, constantly putting themselves at risk, and challenging their environment, to ease the plight and improve the quality of life of others, with whom they have no connection, except their shared humanity. It is noteworthy that those people in whom the Bodhisattva life state is dominant often receive very little public reward or recognition for their work and may pass much of their lives in relatively poor circumstances. Recognition or reward is clearly not their motivation. They are driven by a powerful compassion to ease the plight and raise the life state of others. That is the source of their greatest joy and fulfilment, and it clearly brings it's own reward. In giving more of themselves, they become most themselves.

Buddhism teaches however that the Bodhisattva state should not be self-sacrificial, in the sense of neglecting one's own welfare. The care of others is best delivered, it suggests, by someone who remains strongly aware of their own basic needs and who takes care of their own welfare. In order to give to others most effectively, we have to develop our own strongest and most resilient life state.

Buddhahood

Buddhahood is described as the highest state of life of which human beings are capable. No more, but equally, no less. It is a name or a title that is, of course, overlaid by a huge amount of misconception and misunderstanding, so that it can be very difficult for us to believe that it is a state of life that can be attained by ordinary people, going about their ordinary daily lives. The sort of people we meet on the bus or the train every day for example. But we shouldn't allow that little local difficulty to put us off. Nichiren Daishonin faced very much the same problem. In his time also, Buddhahood meant essentially the state of life that had been achieved by Shakyamuni Buddha in the remote past, who was widely held to be a virtually divine figure.

It was Nichiren, through his intense study of Buddhist writings back through the centuries, including Shakyamuni's own words, who brought Buddhahood back down to earth, so to speak. He made it clear that Shakyamuni was, at all times, an ordinary man, albeit a man of extraordinary wisdom, who had become awakened to the true nature of life. Indeed his greatness, Nichiren wrote, lay precisely in his *"behaviour as a human being."*

Nichiren made it clear that Shakyamuni's awakening was not in any way a superhuman state, in some way elevated above ordinary human life. Nor was it a transcendental state, some place of heavenly peace and tranquillity, cut off from the down-to-earth reality of daily life. This is the key understanding that Nichiren goes to great lengths to explain to us, again and again, throughout his teaching life. Buddhahood is not presented as an elevation of some kind, a higher plane or level of life onto which we might step, as if we were casting off our ordinary lives. It is rather a deeper and a richer understanding of the mainstream of our life, as it already *is*, so that everything we are involved in, the ordinary things, the boring and mundane things, even the suffering and the struggling things, we can experience as happiness.

Living The Ten Worlds

Do the ten worlds match up against the reality of our lives? It doesn't take very much self analysis, I suggest, to recognize in our daily experience the life states they describe, from Hell and Hunger to Learning and Realization and Bodhisattva.

There is no barrier between them. We move from one to the other with great rapidity and with complete freedom, dependant upon what is going on in our lives and in our environment from moment to moment. Nichiren Buddhism describes this fluency of movement from one to the other, by saying that each life state contains all the others. That is to say, we may at this moment be in the life state of Humanity, pretty much at peace with the world, but all the other states are latent within us. We can move in a flash to Anger, or to Bodhisattva, or indeed both in quick succession; anger for example that a stream of car drivers won't stop to let an old man who is clearly unsure of himself, across the road; and then stopping and getting out of your car and taking his arm to ensure that he gets across safely.

If you think about that sort of juxtaposition even briefly, if we weren't offered some such concept, we would have to invent one, to explain the immensely changeable and often contradictory behaviour all of us demonstrate or experience in our lives.

We may not be accustomed to calling these variable and fluc-tuating states of mind," life states" or "worlds," as Buddhism describes them, indeed we take them so much for granted that we may not dignify them with any name at all, but we recognize them rapidly enough when we experience them, or when we have them pointed out to us.

If we are prepared to accept that argument, what follows from it is very important indeed in terms of our understand-ing of Nichiren Buddhism. Indeed it brings us to the central promise made by Nichiren, namely that it is possible for us to experience Buddhahood *in this lifetime*, whatever situation our life happens to be in at any given moment. We have within us, that is, the potential to move from the despair of Hell say, to the compassion of Bodhisattva, or the profound hope and optimism of Buddhahood.

The Normality of Buddhahood

This is the basis for the fundamental argument that has already been touched upon more than once, namely that Buddhahood is not in any way *a superhuman* life state, but a supremely *human* one. It contains within it all the ordinary human life states. Shakyamuni and Nichiren Daishonin were ordinary men who nevertheless attained the highest life state, during their normal life spans on earth. Thus the great promise at the heart of Nichiren Buddhism is that Buddhahood is not some remote and inaccessible goal that can only be attained after several lifetimes of endeavour. It is the immediate, earthly purpose of our daily practice.

Indeed, the key implication is that Buddhahood can *only* exist in the presence of the other nine worlds, it can *only* find expression that is, in the behaviour of ordinary people. Us. What that means is that all of the ten worlds, including the lower worlds of hell and hunger and anger and animality, are *permanently* part of our lives. We can't eliminate them or drive them out in some way. They are part of everyone's life. What we need to do, if we wish to build a happier life for ourselves and those around us, is to face up to their reality, and to set about transforming them, through our practice, from negative aspects of our life, to positive. This is undoubtedly one of the truly remarkable, life- transforming aspects of Nichiren Buddhism, this teaching that we can take any part of our life about which we have been feeling vaguely uneasy or downright unhappy, even guilty or ashamed, and set about transmuting it, through the practice, into a source of value in our lives. Nothing has to be given up. Nothing has to be abandoned. *Nothing* that can exist in the context of our lives is too difficult to change.

The overwhelming message therefore is one of immense hope and optimism. We can, when we feel at our wits end, and seemingly have nowhere to turn, bring out of nowhere, hope, and the strength and life force of our Buddha nature, to challenge our situation and begin at once, to turn it round.

That is part and parcel of what we mean when we talk about taking responsibility for our life. One interpretation of that word *responsibility*, is precisely, *respond-ability*. That is to say, that we always have the choice as to *how* we respond.

That is why so many people describe the effect of their practice as enabling. They come to feel that it helps them to take more control over their lives, instead of drifting in response to circumstances. In a sense it is a restatement of the analogy of the weightlifter. It is a fact of life that we cannot develop stronger muscles except by lifting heavier weights. From the standpoint of Buddhism, it is equally clear that we cannot grow our inner strength except by overcoming obstacles. As Daisaku Ikeda has expressed it:

"True happiness is not the absence of suffering. You can't have day after day of clear skies. True happiness lies in building a self that stands dignified and indomitable. Happiness does not mean having a life free from all difficulties but that whatever difficulties

arise, without being shaken in the least, you can summon up the unflinching courage and conviction to fight and overcome them."*

The Story of Joanna

"I was living in the depths of the country with my two sons Joseph, who was 4 and Gupi who was just a tiny baby, six weeks old. Their father and I had split up when I was several months pregnant, and I had moved to the country with them. I felt very alone and abandoned and I suppose, pretty sorry for myself.

One day a friend whom I had not seen for some time turned up. She started to tell me about Nichiren Buddhism and about how it might help me in my situation. Although I wasn't in the least bit keen I found I had nothing in my own life to meet her arguments with, so, more to shut her up than anything else, I agreed to give it a try. I promised that I would chant for 10 minutes a day, for a whole 100 days.

At the time I couldn't really believe that I had said that. But I had, and being a determined sort of person I kept at it, just as I kept to my routine of running at 6:30 every morning, rain or shine, with Joseph and Gupi in the push chair. In a sense I saw it very much in the same light. I now had two routines, my early morning run and my ten minutes of chanting. From the very beginning the chanting felt natural enough, but strange. In fact to tell the truth I felt a bit mad that I was doing something so unlike myself, and I kept on doing it mainly because I had said I would. But gradually, I did feel different. It is quite difficult to describe it exactly in words, but it was as if the haze dropped away, as if I saw things more clearly. My life generally seemed less daunting, and somehow brighter and clearer. I began to feel that chanting could possibly help me to achieve what I wanted from my life.

The ten minutes a day became forty, and I began to go to meetings, although to be honest I felt that I had nothing much in common with the people I encountered there. Later on I was to feel so grateful to those same people from whom I had at first felt so distant. They became very close to me and supported me in a way that I have never before experienced in my life.

How I felt about my personal life situation began to change fundamentally. I had, I realized always been somewhat spoilt and privileged. And when I found myself poor and abandoned, with no one to help or support me I felt extremely hard done by; that life had treated me badly. That had been my main reaction. I was extremely unhappy, but too proud and reserved to open up to people and ask for help. I just accepted my unhappiness for what it was, and got on with things. As I continued to practice however, I came to see things very differently. I realized that no one owed me anything, and that it was entirely up to me to take responsibility for my life as it now was.

I continued to practice for the stability it brought into my life, and then Gupi, my little boy, now 4, suddenly became very ill. He had severe stomach pains that would not go away. Although one doctor believed that he was just suffering from an intestinal infection, and that it would soon clear up, the pains were so severe that I sought a second opinion. Gupi was immediately referred to the local hospital. We spent a night there that I shall never forget. Gupi passed the night in pain, while I chanted continually beside him.

A scan revealed that he had several tumours in one of his kidneys. We were transferred immediately by ambulance to the main regional hospital where, utterly weary and hungry by now, he had again to put up with being poked and prodded and scanned and x-rayed. The diagnosis was both good and bad. Gupi, the specialist said, did indeed have cancer, but it was of a type that offered a 98% chance of being cured, through chemotherapy. I was in a state of shock. I opened the window for a breath of air I remember, and thought about the long history of medical illness and tragic death in our family. I wasn't going to allow that to happen to Gupi. Gupi was going to *beat* that family karma.

He started his treatment straightaway. He was pumped full of chemicals through a tube in his hand, while he insisted on watching. He said that he had to see what was happening otherwise he would be too frightened. Throughout the week Nichiren Buddhists from the local area came to support me and chanted with me for hours in the room at the hospital. I felt immensely supported, and chanting had become my lifeline. After that week he was allowed home and had to return to hospital once a week for chemotherapy. But it wasn't long before it became clear that things were getting worse and that he would have to have an operation to remove the tumour. I was told that it was possible that he could die during this operation.

A group of us chanted throughout the operation with every ounce of our courage. I was so frightened that when they came to tell me the results my ears simply couldn't hear what they were saying. Eventually I realized that they were trying to tell me that it had gone well. When I think back to that time one of the things that sticks in my memory is just how strong and positive we were, despite all that was going on. Visitors who passed the room would look in and say, "Can we come in? It's so lovely in here." There was a very special, bright feeling in that little room. I remember it with such pleasure, even though Gupi was going through such a severe treatment. And, as though he was picking up on our positive thoughts, he himself never lost his spirits. I have this image of him skipping along the corridor.

After that we had a three months respite at home. Gupi seemed a little stronger. Then a check scan revealed a lump in the cavity where the kidney had been. I feared what the tests would show. The cancer had returned with a vengeance. I was told that there was nothing more that could be done for him.

I felt utterly trapped. But not beaten. I had a fierce anger against this negativity that had attacked our lives. I felt like a warrior; there was no way that I was going to give in. I determined to chant seven hours a day to challenge it. It was immensely difficult. When I made the determination I didn't see how I could possibly achieve it. I would get up at 3 am in the dark and go to the Gohonzon to summon up my strength. This went on for over 3 months. Many people came to chant with us, and there was constant support from local members of SGI. Gupi began to show signs of recovery. He even became well enough to go back to school. When he was picked up from school he would sometimes run along the lane trying to beat the car.

"How could he die of this?" I thought. He used to ask me *"Could this tumour kill me?"* It could, "I replied, *"but we're not going to let it."*

But he had another scan and the doctor said that he did not know what was keeping him alive. Gupi died quickly one morning sitting up in his bed. He was looking at me. Then he died.

The day of Gupi's funeral was the proudest day of my life. I felt that I still had him in my hands, my beautiful, perfect child, that he was like a helium balloon, high in the sky, but still attached to me.

The chanting at his funeral was extraordinary, with an incredible dynamic rhythm. As his coffin disappeared I wasn't hysterical. I just felt an overwhelming sense of gratitude that I had been his mother, and that I had been so close to this amazing person with the heart of a lion. He took me to places I would never have dared to go on my own. Because of what I went through with him I know that there is nothing that I cannot face. I understand human suffering. I know now that the experience that Gupi and I went through together was my good fortune. I began practicing Buddhism when he was just 6 weeks old, and I know that I have him to thank. I am emotional still, and problems have by no means vanished from my life. But I'm not at the mercy of my emotions; the person I used to be still exists within me but I am aware of a greater, wiser self."

CHAPTER SEVEN

What is Karma All About?

There is a close connection between the fundamental life states that we have been discussing in the previous chapter, and the somewhat elusive concept of karma. Thus although we all possess within our lives, all of these ten life states, as you might expect, we all manifest them in a way that is unique to us. That is to say we all experience them in different combinations and with different degrees of intensity. But a key point is that Buddhism teaches that our lives tend to be dominated by just *one* of these states. We still experience all of them, and shift rapidly from one to another from moment to moment, as we go through the day, but Buddhism teaches that we tend to inhabit one or perhaps two of them with much greater frequency than the others. All that is saying in effect, is that we have dominant characteristics, or as Buddhism describes it, a dominant life tendency.

Does that ring true in our personal experience of life? If we think about it even for a moment, we can recognize its validity in the sense that we often tend to see other people, essentially in terms of a dominant characteristic in their make up. We all know people whom we think of primarily as having a short fuse and being quick to anger or argument, while others seem to have a naturally outgoing and sunny temperament, no matter what fuss and bother is going on around them. There are some we know who always seem to find the time and the space in their lives, to put themselves out to quite extraordinary lengths, to help and assist other people. Others are somehow more shut off, living very much within themselves and not often given to outward shows of emotion.

Buddhism explains that this fundamental or dominant tendency in all our lives, that has such a key role to play in everything about us; how we think, how we respond to circumstances, even the expression on our face, is in some measure, a manifestation of our karma.

So What is Karma?

The concept of karma is taken very much for granted by at least half the population of the world, mainly in Asia. In the West however, although it is probably the Buddhist term that is most widely used, it is also the one that is probably most widely misused, understandably enough perhaps, because it is quite a difficult concept to pin down. It is often described in the West as having to do with destiny, for example, or with fate, in the general sense of something that is inevitable and that we cannot avoid. If that were the case, it would of course have a profound effect upon the professed purpose of Buddhism, to enable us to change, and to learn how to live the most creative and fulfilled lives of which we are capable.

The concept of karma goes back to the very roots of human civilisation in the East, long before Shakyamuni's time. That is indicated by the fact that the word itself comes from the ancient Sanskrit language, a word that originally meant not fate or destiny but *action*. So in Buddhism, it is the term used to describe the chain of actions, or the chain of causes and effects, that runs through all of our lives. It represents, if you like, the constant link between the past, the present and future. It links all the actions or causes that have been made in the past, with the effects that continue to have a powerful influence on our life in the present, and will continue to do so, on into the future.

It goes without saying that everyone, without exception, has karma. We create it all the time with everything that we do, which is taken to include not just actual deeds, but our thoughts and words as well. We can think generally in terms of both *good* karma, created for example, by acts of compassion towards others, or courage in the face of difficulty, and *bad or negative* karma created for example by slandering somebody, or simply being totally thoughtless and having no concern for the effect of our actions on others. Damaging actions create much heavier karma than angry words, and angry words heavier karma than hostile or aggressive thoughts, that never get translated into words or actions.

As we make this continuous stream of causes, we are, according to the Buddhist view of cause and effect, simultaneously laying down, or planting in our lives, seeds; effects that will manifest themselves at some time in the future, when the external conditions are right. So *every* action we take leads to a future action in an unbroken chain. That, in brief, is our karma. The sum total in a sense, of all the causes and effects that we have generated in our lives. Not fate. Not destiny. Not pre-ordained. There is no external power in Buddhism remember, who could in any sense pre-ordain our fate. *We* create our own karma by the way *we* choose to live.

That is why we often talk about karma in terms of *habit*, or habitual patterns of thought and behaviour. Confronted with similar circumstances we tend to react in a similar way, because of our karmic or *dominant* life tendency. People who know us at all well can often predict pretty closely how we are going to behave or respond to a given set of circumstances. They might even look out for it, or make something of a joke of just how predictable we are. We often berate ourselves, for example, when we think back over something we have just done, and wonder how on earth we could have repeated the same, silly error of judgement, in just the same sort of way. How often do we cringe with embarrassment when we have a moment to reflect on a response we have made or an action we have taken? We may excuse ourselves for having made it perhaps, on the spur of the moment, without time to consider, but that of course is precisely the point. In responding in that particular way, we revealed something inherent in our nature. Similarly, people will frequently describe how successive relationships in their lives, often with very similar types of people, have come to an end, having followed an almost identical trajectory.

Karma is Us

Thus the concept of karma seeks to teach us above all that no one is responsible for our karma, except ourselves. There is nothing to be gained from blaming others. Indeed that can only lead to similar sequences of events occurring again, because it means in essence that we are denying our responsibility for whatever it is that happened, and so setting ourselves up to repeat the same sort of actions. It is, if you like, an integral part of our lives, an essential part of who we are now, today. We cannot see it or feel it of course, this karma, so we tend to ignore it. But it is ours, just as clearly as our face and figure are ours, and in a similar way, both can reveal the accumulated history of our lives.

We take it with us wherever we go, rather like a rucksack on our back. We can't so to speak, sell up and move across to the other side of the world and leave it all behind with the rest of our house furniture, and hope to start all over again. Well we can of course, but we can't leave the causes and effects behind, with the settees and the sideboards. We carry with us our dominant life tendency, and the latent effects of all the causes that we have made hitherto, which will be expressed in action when the appropriate set of external circumstances comes along. In that sense it is wholly accurate when people talk about the chains, or the shackles of our karma. All that is really saying of course, is that we can't escape from *ourselves.* We all know from our own experience, just how deeply, past actions, good and bad and indifferent, are inscribed in the fabric of our lives, and still have a profound resonance in our lives today. Karma, in essence, is just putting a Buddhist name to that knowledge.

It embodies the truth that causes and the effects arise from within, and if there are things about our life that repeatedly cause us pain and grief, then changing our circumstances in some cosmetic way cannot have a lasting effect. Just as changing our clothes may marginally alter our appearance, but it cannot have a lasting effect upon our behaviour. To achieve real change we have to set about changing, with the help of our Buddhist practice, the dominant life tendency that lies at the root of our troubles. We have to change within.

When we are talking about moving across the world it's also important to remember that, in Buddhist terms, we carry our environment with us. All that means is that, our dominant life tendency will attract that same tendency from our environment, wherever we happen to end up. Compassion within will continue to attract compassion without, just as anger within will attract anger without.

The key point however, and one that cannot be emphasised too strongly, is that karma is not in any way an outside force somehow bearing down upon our lives, which we can't avoid. That, strictly speaking, is fatalism. The message of Buddhism by contrast is infinitely more positive and constructive, since it is about personal responsibility. We create karma as a result of our own actions. We are therefore, both entirely responsible for it, and, Buddhism argues, we have within us, the power to change it.

The critical starting point for any change is self awareness. That is already a huge step forward. It is a bit like equipping ourselves with a far better pair of spectacles. It suddenly brings everything into sharper focus. We become aware that our actions and decisions are not *determined* by our karmic tendencies, just profoundly influenced by them. Thus when Peter starts an aggressive row with Paul say, it may be that Paul's dominant life tendency of Anger would normally push him towards direct retaliation in kind. But the *awareness* of what is really happening in the situation, may provide just sufficient pause, for judgement to come into play, to allow Paul to break the cycle. Instead of reacting to aggression, karmically, you might say, with the bad cause of a slanging match, he deflects Peter's aggression with a humorous remark say, and restores the mood to one of good humoured argument. If that were to happen of course friends of both who were standing by watching the exchange, might well comment on this "new and unexpected side" to Paul's character. He has changed that is, his habitual, pattern of behaviour.

However, awareness by itself cannot of course be enough to change deeply rooted karmic tendencies. Buddhism teaches that it is really only through the consistent and steady discipline of the daily practice, that we can move our lives forward, from the essentially reactive states such as Anger and Hunger towards, the proactive life states of Learning and Realisation and Bodhisattva and Buddhahood. One of the meanings attached to the process of chanting is "to summon up." Changing karma undoubtedly involves summoning up, with all our strength, the power of our Buddha nature.

The Dilemma of Inherited Karma

Buddhism teaches that our life entity goes through successive periods of active, waking life on this earth, and periods of latency. Perhaps the nearest comparison that can be made to this idea, is the periods of waking and sleeping that we experience every day. Each waking day contains within it the potential for the sleep that is to come. Each period of sleep has within it the potential for the re-awakening that is to come. The idea of successive periods of active life raises the fundamental question of precisely which "bit" of us goes on from active life to active life? That is the issue we discuss at greater length in Chapter 14.

The key issue, with which we are specifically concerned here, is that Buddhism teaches that karma is handed on from one period of active life to the next. In fact Buddhism teaches that *all* the accumulated effects from *all* previous periods of active life, without exception, are carried forward to the next life.

The essential dilemma, moral dilemma if you will, that the teaching of inherited karma presents is that if we have not the slightest memory of actions in previous lives, in what sense can we be held responsible for them in this one? That is the nub of the problem we have to wrestle with.

It is undoubtedly difficult in the extreme for most people who have not been born into a Buddhist or a Hindu culture, to accept the idea, that not only are we born with karma, but that the karma attaching to unremembered actions in previous lives, has played a role in determining the physical circumstances of our life. That it is no less, offered as an explanation of sorts, for all the differences in advantage and disadvantage, health, wealth, even in choice of parents. Among many other things it might well offend our sense of justice and equity. How can we be saddled, from birth, we might ask, with the effects that were incurred by someone whom we don't know and can't remember?

The short answer from Buddhism might well be that it did not *create* this concept of karma, and the truth of it's inheritance. It isn't simply an intellectual theory, a sort of virtual construct. It is, Buddhism argues, an observation. *This is the way things are*, in very much the same way that the physical laws of the Universe are not *created* by scientists, but simply observed, and described by them, as they learn more and more about the way the world works.

Sitting in his little office in Berne, for example Einstein did not simply *invent* his famous equation, $e=mc2$, that describes the extraordinary, mind-boggling relationship between energy and matter that applies throughout the entire universe. He observed it with his mind. Similarly, Buddhism would argue, Shakyamuni, seeking to understand the lives of the people around him, didn't invent the law of inherited karma, he observed it as a fundamental truth.

He could no more modify it, to render it more palatable than he could fly by flapping his arms. He remained subject to the law of gravity!

So What are the Options?

That leaves us with the option of course, of either accepting the Buddhist view as a meaningful representation of our lives, or not. That doesn't mean that it will go away of course, but it does pose the question, what other options are there, to help us account for the vast differences in the circumstances of people's lives? What alternatives are there to explain for us, the deep mystery of human pain and suffering, that very often appears to be totally random and undeserved, and that can run continually almost from birth to death in many people's lives.

These are questions of course that in many ways are simply unanswerable. They lie genuinely beyond our comprehension, and this is simply not the place for an extended philosophical debate. But if we were to seek some sort of answer, it seems that there are precious few options to choose from. Let us list them briefly. From my reading and research, I can only think of three.

The first is that the pain and the suffering have been created, along with everything else that makes up the universe, by an all- powerful, creator God or gods. It's an argument that leaves us with the problem of explaining how or why it is, that God has created the evil of suffering that people can experience from their earliest days on Earth, alongside the good of his mercy. But it would I believe, represent a perfectly logical extension of what is held to be the case in the Abrahamic religions.

However, if one does not believe in the existence of an all-powerful creator God, it clearly is not available to us as an explanation.

The second option might be that suffering of this nature is simply a matter of chance, pure bad luck, inexplicable in any rational sense. Simply a matter of a random throw of the dice. Some people are fortunate enough to have good luck, others have bad. That, if you like, is all there is to it. I think it's likely that the vast majority of people, if they were to examine their position, would sit within this camp; there is no rational explanation to offer for the vast differences in the circumstances of people's lives, it's purely a matter of chance. Again this is a logical position, although that is about the most that can be said for it. In human terms it is entirely without hope or consolation, and human beings without hope are in a desperate and desolate situation.

The third option is the Buddhist view or something close to it, which we have discussed. It seeks to establish a *direct* connection of individual responsibility, between suffering that is experienced at any stage in life, and causes or actions that have been taken, at some earlier stage, by the responsible individual.

At first glance, as we have seen, it might seem immensely unjust, because Buddhism teaches that that responsibility can be carried across from one period of active life to the next, without a continuation of memory. But from a slightly different perspective, it also carries with it a great message of hope, in two main ways. One is that it eliminates the idea of randomness and chaos in the occurrence of suffering, that can be so unsettling and disturbing to the human mind, in fact a major cause of suffering in itself. Mankind has worked hard over the centuries to evolve societies based on principles of individual responsibility and fairness and justice, because these factors are fundamental to our sense of balance and well being. We hate the idea of randomness and chaos.

The second, and perhaps the most important point, is that the Buddhist proposition offers the chance of restoration, of taking action to create a change in the situation, taking action that is, to overcome the suffering, and create a new direction in life.

It is not of course for me to argue here, the case for the first two options, the all powerful God as a source of suffering as well as good, or the role of chance in life. Those have to be personal choices. But what is the action that we can take as Nichiren Buddhists?

Can we Change Karma?

This is in many ways the ultimate question, since it is asking whether or not we can transform fundamentally, those parts of our life that are causing us to suffer. And in the final analysis, *all* Buddhist teachings are focused on responding to that question, in the sense of enabling fundamental change in our lives at many levels; changing unhappy karma, changing circumstances to increase the sum total of well being in our lives, and changing those things that hold us back from fulfilling our potential.

Thus at the very heart of Nichiren Buddhism lies this affirmation that karma is about the *future* of our lives, as well as the past. The future it argues, is created from this moment on, in the causes that we start to make now. Thus it is a message of the greatest hope and optimism. It assures us that, although the law of cause and effect is immutable, in the sense that we will, inevitably, at some point in the future, experience the effects of harmful or damaging causes we have made in the past, the actions that we take from now on, can change and alleviate the way those effects appear in our lives. That is true, we are assured, even of deep seated fundamental karma, which might give rise to great or long continued pain in our lives.

It teaches that the most powerful good cause that we can make is undoubtedly chanting, and taking action based on the wisdom and the courage and the compassion that it brings out in us. In this way, we are promised, we can begin to break out of the habits and patterns of behaviour that have become established in our life, that continue to cause us grief. Buddhism talks about moving from our lesser self to our greater or essential self. We don't necessarily have to use that sort of language. We know, or most of us know, that we have a meaner and narrower side to our character that gets us involved in all sorts of things that we are not particularly proud of, and wouldn't want to write home about. Conversely we have a more open and generous, and outgoing dimension to our lives that gets us involved in the kinds of things that make us feel good about ourselves. The promise is that the practice of chanting, moves us steadily away from the meaner self, towards the stronger and more resilient self, awakening, summoning up, our Buddha nature.

It is in the enthusiastic and energetic commitment to the daily practice then, that we find the key to changing unhappy karma.

We set rolling in our lives if you like, a wheel, a virtuous circle, and as it gathers momentum, it can lead to a transformation in the very broadest sense, in the way we handle our relationships, in the way we relate to our environment and the way our environment responds to us.

From Negative to Positive

So what started out as a seemingly negative proposition, can be seen to contain within it the potential for a very positive outcome. Moreover, the more we challenge our own negative karma, and feel the effects of that, the more life energy we have left over to help others who are less fortunate, to challenge theirs. Practising that is, for ourselves and others. The beneficial effects of that cannot be over stated, since it is the nexus that lies at the very heart of Buddhism.

As the old adage has it, give a starving man a fish and you feed him for a day. Give him a fishing rod, and you can feed him for life. The practice of Nichiren Buddhism in this context, might be seen as the spiritual fishing rod.

Thus Buddhism argues that in the final analysis, merely seeking *our own* happiness can never be enough. "No man is an island." We can never isolate ourselves from what is going on in other people's lives, no matter how strongly we may believe, or try to convince ourselves, that we can. Lasting and indestructible happiness, of the kind that we are all seeking, can only come from working wherever we spot an opportunity, to create value and good fortune and harmony, not only in our own lives, but in the lives of all those with whom we come in contact.

It is a unquestionably a long journey, to travel from dealing with our own negative karma, to thinking about the peace of the world, but it is the journey Buddhism asks us to travel. The circle of our fellow human beings does not of course, end with the company of our family, or our friends, or our village or our town. It travels out to the limits of mankind, and the ultimate goal of the SGI, the lay Buddhist organisation which is based entirely on the Buddhism of Nichiren Daishonin, is nothing less than world peace.

On the face of it that may seem to be a fruitless and an impossible task, well beyond anyone's capacity. But Buddhism asks us not to allow ourselves to be limited and hemmed in by our nameless fears and the narrowness of our vision.

That happens to be a view that has been shared by many inspirational leaders down the years.

John F. Kennedy, for example, in his Commencement Address, made in June 1963, provided a clear vision of what that broader, infinitely bolder and more positive approach might deliver. He declared;

"First examine our attitude towards peace itself. Too many of us think it impossible, too many think it is unreal, but that is a dangerous, defeatist belief. It leads to the conclusion that war is inevitable, that mankind is doomed, that we are gripped by forces we cannot control. We need not accept that view. Our problems are man-made, therefore, they can be solved by man, and man can be as big as he wants. No problem of human destiny is beyond human beings. Man's reason and spirit have often solved the seemingly unsolvable, and we believe we can do it again."

World peace might seem to be an unattainable goal, but it starts, we come to realize, within our own lives and within the circle of our immediate environment. Basically it is about how we relate to others around us, and that is where we move to in the next chapter.

CHAPTER EIGHT

A Question of Relationships

As we have touched upon earlier, there has been a huge amount of research over the past decade or so seeking to define what makes people feel good about themselves. What kinds of things do people have in their minds when they are thinking about a sense of completeness or well-being?

It comes as something of surprise perhaps, in such an aggressively materialistic age, that wealth doesn't seem to feature very strongly as a factor. Although money is obviously a very necessary ingredient in our lives, beyond a certain point, quite a low point in fact, it doesn't seem to contribute a great deal as far as happiness is concerned. What is encouraging is that many of the themes that we have been talking about in these pages do have a strong presence in the research results. A greater sense of control over one's own life, for example, is undoubtedly a supremely important ingredient. Few things, it seems, are as demoralising as the feeling that most of the key elements in one's life are somehow beyond one's control. A strong sense of self worth is also seen to be a powerful factor in coping with the chaotic and the unpredictable events in our life, and hence immensely liberating.

But one crucial factor that underlies many others would seem to be a sense of connectedness, of not being locked into the narrow concerns of our own life, but having a sense of belonging to a wider group or community.

Daisaku Ikeda has expressed something very similar;

*"To be filled each day with a rewarding sense of exhilaration and purpose, a sense of tasks accomplished and deep fulfilment; people who feel this way are happy. Of course the mission or objective that you have taken on yourself, must be in accord with the happiness of oneself and others. That is what makes absolute happiness possible."**

"Oneself and others." It is the essential phrase that appears again and again in Buddhist writings, this belief underlying Buddhist practice, that unshakeable happiness for ourselves is only to be found in the context of a compassionate concern for happiness and growth in the lives of others.

The research really confirms what is a common factor in our daily experience, namely that we are, in our deepest nature, a gregarious animal. We earnestly seek lasting and fulfilling and harmonious relationships at all levels in our lives. When we achieve them at home and at work for example, two of the most important environments, they buttress and reinforce our creative energies. We become freed, so to speak, to pursue many other outward objectives in our lives. When those relationships break down for whatever reason, the effects can be devastating in all the areas of our life, not simply those associated with the relationship that has gone wrong, but everywhere. We operate as individuals under stress, and that stress is reflected back at us from all our environments.

When relationships at work for example are difficult and stressful, they can lead all too rapidly to argument and discord at home, and even trigger the break down of a relationship. In the same way, the break-up of a long-term relationship with a partner, even when it is achieved by mutual agreement, undoubtedly sends out tremors and shock waves into every corner of our social and working life.

Since relationships therefore are central to the growth and development of all human lives it can be no surprise that they are also central to Buddhist teaching. Although Buddhist practice is aimed in every way, at building a strong, resilient inner self, it is fundamentally an outgoing activity. It is not expressed in isolation, inside our head as it were. It only becomes meaningful as something that is lived in society. The real significance we are told, of Shakyamuni's teaching, was expressed in his *behaviour as a human being*. Buddhism basically describes our lives as being lived in three overlapping realms or areas; specifically us or the self, at the centre, then society or other people, then the wider all embracing environment. In order to achieve full and satisfying lives, we have to build good, strong relationships in all three areas.

So the daily struggle to *live* as a Buddhist, and let's be clear, it does require real determination,, rather than simply to know and understand Buddhist principles, becomes apparent above all, in the way we handle the countless relationships that occur at every level in our lives, throughout each day. Relationships in the very broadest sense, embracing all the encounters, all the people you bump into, as you move through the day, from getting up with   your partner and getting the kids off to school perhaps, to ticket sellers and travelling companions and work colleagues and clients and strangers, and on and on, throughout the day.

Buddhism teaches that the way in which we handle each of those encounters, has far wider and deeper implications than simply the reverberations that we experience in our own life. So how should we handle them? What specifically does Buddhism have to tell us about creating the greatest value out of all those encounters?

What do we Mean by Respect?

Right at the top of the list comes the idea of respect. It is in some ways an old fashioned word. It could certainly be argued that it was valued and lived by an older generation more readily than it is by today's. Politicians of every persuasion and in many countries, frequently express the view that many of the most challenging problems facing modern societies arise because of its relative absence, the widespread lack of regard for the dignity and humanity of other people.

It is a central pillar of Buddhist thought. What it comes down to is that, if we want to live in a society that is based fundamentally on respect for the individual, then *we* have to demonstrate that respect as a core quality in all our relationships and encounters. We are not required to like people, or indeed to admire them. We do have to dig deep, whatever the circumstances, and recognize their common humanity Shakyamuni and Nichiren Daishonin, both had profoundly revolutionary visions of the way in which societies should work, based on each person learning how to respect *every other* human being with whom they came in contact, whatever the circumstances. It was revolutionary then. When it is expressed in these stark terms it's clear that it is still revolutionary today.

But it is the heart of the matter. Buddhism is based on freedom of choice. Thus it argues that the way in which we experience a relationship is also a matter of choice. We have the power that is, to choose whether we experience any particular relationship in a negative or a positive way. It is of course all too easy for us to fasten on what we feel to be the errors and the inconsistencies and irrationalities of other people's behaviour that make relationships difficult or inconvenient for *us*. All those things that make them seemingly unattractive or objectionable, to *us*. Different from us. Other. Not part of the way we want our world to be.

If we leave aside the wider world for a moment, I am very much aware from my own behaviour for example, that it is all too easy to slip into patterns of behaviour that are basically disrespectful, even with people who are very close to us, even with people we love and seek to protect. We can find ourselves disrespecting them in the sense of using them to achieve our own goals, or disregarding their needs. The tendency to use other people for what we see as our own vitally important ends, seems to be very strongly embedded in human nature. So the battle, Buddhism teaches, starts within our own lives, within our own very close environment. And Buddhism makes it clear that it *is* a battle, a struggle between the inclination to diminish and use other human beings, and the intellectual understanding that we should respect them.

There is no easy path. This is very much the process of human revolution that each one of us becomes involved in as a practising Buddhist. There is no point in taking part in a demonstration say, to shout against the abuses of human rights in a distant African state, or march with a million other people down the Strand against war in Iraq, if we are not demonstrating that respect for others in every way in our own lives. The daily Buddhist practice is the route, first to awareness, and then to strengthening and confirming our determination to get better at it.

The Reality of Responsibility

We have touched upon this idea several times before, but it is central to the Buddhist view of building relationships, namely accepting responsibility for our own lives.

It is a nicely rounded phrase, "accepting responsibility for our own lives." It rolls smoothly of the tongue. But its very familiarity can make it deceptive. When relationships don't work, for example, for whatever reason, we often, and quite instinctively, seek to locate the cause outside ourselves We might go on the defensive for example; it doesn't work, we say, because of something they have done, or something in their nature that is unacceptable or illogical. That *must* be the root cause. In my experience it is uncommonly difficult to accept the Buddhist dictum that the problem can't be resolved simply by looking for the other person to change, until they meet our specification, so to speak. However much that might seem to us to be the *obvious* way forward, getting *them* to change for the better, Buddhism awkwardly teaches us that the reverse is true.

The key understanding that we have to work hard to achieve, is that we are not, and cannot be, responsible for the behaviour of others, however close they are to us, however well we know them, however much we love them. We can only be responsible for our own behaviour. So, if *we* are suffering, it is *our* problem to solve, and the solution can only lie with us, not with someone else. If that were the case we would be handing over to someone else, responsibility for our own life. That is of course childhood, rather than adulthood, weakness rather than strength.

We have all been through this sort of circumstance many times over. We are hurt or offended, or in some way put out by another person, at home or at work for example. It is perfectly natural for us to withdraw within our defences to protect ourselves. That's what defences are for, withdrawing behind! And then we begin to list all the faults in the other person that have clearly led to the hurt or the offence. From then on the solution seems simple; we simply have to get this other person to change in this way or that and then we'll be happy. Simple. We might even go so far as to work out strategies for ensuring that the changes in the other person take place. We all know that people do go to extraordinary efforts to change the behaviour of others, in an effort to make relationships work. We might even persuade ourselves that the changes have taken place so that just about everything in the other person is now fixed to *our* satisfaction. And when the original behaviour reasserts itself, it can lead to even greater frustration. What went wrong? Why has the other person let us down yet again, in this thoughtless way?

I've been there, many times.

Moreover, as we know to our cost, it doesn't stop at one relationship. Experience shows that the pattern repeats itself. We are back to karma, and the dominant life tendency. It is very often the case that people move off to a new place, or a new job or a new relationship, and very similar sequences of events take place. Why? In relationships, as in everything else, we like to think that by changing people or changing locations, we can simply move on, and start all over again as if nothing had happened. It is undoubtedly one of the most difficult lessons to learn that we have to deal with the causes we have made. We can't somehow run away from them, any more than we can run away from our physical appearance. They are both part of our life.

The only person whose patterns of thought and action we can control is ourselves, however much we may wish to think otherwise. If we are seeking to change others, then we may have a long time to wait. In Buddhism therefore, one of the key understandings about building and maintaining strong relationships, is that the effort to make things work out, the action to change things about our relationship that cause us pain or suffering or recurring difficulty has to come from within ourselves.

Independence Works

There is another related issue that is very important in close and loving relationships. It has to do with the idea of dependency. Putting it at its simplest, Buddhism teaches that our ability to be happy in our lives is a matter of choice. Our choice. It has, or should have, nothing to do with anyone or anything outside of ourselves, even those who are supremely close to us. As Daisaku Ikeda has expressed it,

*"Happiness is not something that someone else, like a lover, can give to us. We have to achieve it for ourselves."**

It is therefore our deal, it has solely to do with how we choose to perceive and to respond to the daily circumstances and vicissitudes of our life, the ups and the downs, the bumps and the knocks that we all experience.

When things are going swimmingly there is generally no problem. When things become troublesome we have the choice, either to use these problematic circumstances as a kind of justification for our failure, or our sadness, or alternatively, to see them as the catalyst for our growth. The nature of the choice we make affects both how we feel and the quality of our life during the episode itself, and during it's aftermath. Is it positive or is it negative? Is it happy or is it sad? No one does it to us, we do it to ourselves, we have the choice.

If we now transfer that thought to this arena of close and loving relationships, it has a profound effect upon how we perceive them, and how we might work to make the most of them. If for example, we see our happiness or our fulfilment as an individual, *dependent* upon our partner, that may seem on the face of it, to make us feel closer and more intimately bonded together. But in fact it can only be a recipe for instability and potentially great unhappiness, even if that person happens to love us dearly. It makes our life state at any moment or, more seriously, our sense of self worth, basically dependent upon the shifting highs and lows of someone else's life. We come to see our happiness as largely dependent upon the existence or the behaviour of our partner. We can't be happy without them we tell ourselves. That may sound on the face of it, to be deeply loving, but think about it. It's a bit like being in the driving seat of a car, and giving the steering wheel to someone else to control. That is scarcely a strategy for success in getting from A to B.

A similar point is to be made of course, about another person's relationship with us. If their happiness and sense of self worth is largely dependent upon us, it might make us feel good to be *in control*, so to speak, but it can only be unstable and unsettling in a long- term relationship. It can become such an immense burden, to be responsible for another person's happiness that it can eventually undermine even the strongest loving relationships. That is perhaps one of the reasons why such a high proportion of modern marriages end in divorce, because of sheer strain imposed upon such relationships by wholly unrealistic expectations.

To feel love for another person and to be loved by them is of course a deeply enriching experience and it is undoubtedly what most of us seek. A life without it is very much the poorer. But that having been said, the modern idiom of romantic love, created largely by the Hollywood Dream Factory, initially in those swoony romances of the 1920's and 30's but now very much the common currency, is, by definition unreal. It isn't, and never was intended to be, a reflection of life on the street. It is, of course, romantic nonsense, a form of escapism intended to float us away for an hour or two, from the altogether harsher realities of everyday life. If we choose in any way to walk out of the cinema with it still active in our minds, and confuse it with reality, it can only create a set of wholly unrealistic expectations. Namely, that there is a Mister or Miss Right out there, who *alone* has the power to make us happy. Or that it is the partner's responsibility in the relationship to deliver our personal happiness. *"We've found them at last and now its their job to make us happy!"*

The Power of Gratitude

There is one other quality, prominent in Buddhist teachings, that advances and enriches relationships, in wonderful and constantly surprising ways. It is the quality of gratitude. We've all experienced how just a few words of appreciation, however simple, however direct, can bring an extraordinary warmth and sense of shared humanity into any situation, even the most casual and superficial, over a shop counter for example, or on bus, or responding to a piece of information over the phone. Multiply that dozens, hundreds of times a day in relation to all the encounters we have with other people at every level of intimacy, and you can see that almost without our being aware of it, it can transform the whole tenor of our whole day, and over time, of our whole life. It has such a powerful transforming effect. Everybody benefits, the giver of the gratitude, the receiver, and all those who are in earshot, they all experience a strengthening of their sense of the value of just being alive.

Thus the Buddhist view of successful relationships is very much basic common sense. It goes back to that underlying principle that we alone are responsible for our lives, and the choices that we make. Essentially it argues that in any field of life, in relationships with a partner, or with family and friends and work colleagues alike, the most resilient and satisfying and value-creating relationships cannot be sustained on a basis of mutual dependence, even if they start out that way. They need a clear sense of independence, and awareness of individual responsibility, allied of course to a profound respect for the wholeness of the other person's life.

Recognizing Negativity

So the basic Buddhist approach to all relationships of whatever kind, right across the board of human experience, is based on that central, revolutionary perception by Shakyamuni so long ago, that every human being without exception, has this huge potential of Buddhahood within him or her. And the purpose of the daily practice established by Nichiren is, in a sense to sharpen our recognition of that potential in ourselves and others. Why on a daily basis? Because the negativity in our lives never gives up. It gets up with us every morning, and just as the devil always has the best tunes, so our negativity has some of the most insidious arguments.

It is the little familiar if you like, that sits on our shoulder when we are somewhat uncertain, and whispers in our ear that we can't do it, or that we won't achieve it, or that to avoid failure or embarrassment, we should give up and walk away. Our evil or negative twin, as it has sometimes been called, is a powerful and persuasive advocate, never at rest, always immensely skilled at playing precisely upon our greatest areas of weakness or self-doubt, always most active when we are challenging or trying to change something really important in our lives; to build on a relationship, or aim for a better job, or dig ourselves out of a particularly frustrating situation.

Buddhism teaches that this causes us grief not because we *have* negativity in our make up, but because we are persuaded to *listen* to its arguments, and accept them as representing the reality of our life. Every time we give in, so to speak, we make it harder to challenge our negativity the next time an opportunity presents itself. Until perhaps we find our lives so dominated by negative thoughts that we no longer recognize them for what they are. They become the habitual environment within which we live our lives. Conversely every time we challenge the negativity, we make it easier to recognize it for what it is and overcome it, the next time around.

That essentially is what we mean when we talk about our human revolution; battling against our inherent negativity, and doing so on a daily basis, because it never goes away. Although we tend not to think about ourselves in this way, those negative qualities are a natural and essential part of our humanity. They remain latent within us even when we are feeling at our most positive. Every time we chant, whether we are aware of it or not, we are engaging in that battle to repel and overcome the weaker and the negative and the destructive elements within us.

Buddhism describes these elements in all sorts of ways, as obstacles or illusions or delusions, even as devils and demons. When it talks about devils, or for that matter, about gods, it is simply using that language to give a physical identity to an inner mental state. The demons and gods aren't powers without, they are negative and positive tendencies within. And the fundamental reason why Buddhism uses the language of battle so frequently, is because it takes our negativity so seriously. It recognizes absolutely the immense damage it can do to the quality of our life, constantly limiting and restricting it in various ways. So a hazy, generalised, impersonalised perception of negativity simply isn't good enough. Nichiren for example goes out of his way to give us a detailed portrait of the various forms in which negativity will inevitably show up in our lives, almost as if he were taking us through an identity parade. It looks just like this, and this, and this, he is saying, on the basis that a clear recognition and understanding of the enemy is the essential first line of defence.

The startling paradox of course is that we cannot have the one without the other. We cannot grow and develop the strong and positive side of our nature, unless it has the negative side to push and struggle against. The fitness analogy is very accurate. We know full well that in order to make ourselves physically strong we are going to have to struggle and sweat a bit. No pain, no gain. Very much the same is true of our practice. Thus, overcoming the negative voice is the springboard to our mental strength. That is not of course, one big leap and then we are free. That would be the equivalent of one visit to the gym. It is a continuous process, one small step, one small victory, after another.

But then people walk all the way up to the very pinnacle of Mount Everest, precisely by taking one small step after another.

CHAPTER NINE

Buddhism and The World About Us

Buddhist practice encompasses everything that we do in the course of the day, all the encounters we might have with other people, all the problems and the successes, all the joys and the irritations that come our way. That is not to say that we are necessarily thinking about it as a conscious process, indeed we are extremely unlikely to be. What we are seeking is that our Buddhist values become the essential basis on which we handle all events and respond to all situations.

Needless to say that isn't always so, and the primary purpose of the chanting in the morning is to make that more likely to be the case, to give us the energy and the will to be positive and up-beat about the coming day. Its purpose is to breathe a bit of inspiration and optimism into us before we slam the door and set off down the road, to deal with the people and the events we will encounter.

But there is another less obvious way of describing it, and that would be to say that we are seeking to create a positive environment around ourselves. To put it in that oblique way raises one of the most important ideas that Buddhism teaches, and perhaps one of the most difficult to get our minds round, namely that we *create* our own environment. As we move from place to place, Buddhism argues, we create the environment in which we function. Or to put it slightly more formally, it teaches that there is really no distinction between ourselves and the world around us, so that we and our environment don't simply interact in a number of ways, but that we are completely inseparable, part of the same whole.

This fundamental principle is described as oneness of self and environment. It is unquestionably a huge idea, but one that is quite difficult to get to grips with as a realistic, down to earth proposition. Leaving aside the obvious green issues, the concern not to despoil but to conserve the environment in the conventional sense, the basic question that it gives rise to is, what real difference does it make to the way we see our lives? How significant is it in this basic endeavour to fold positive Buddhist values into our daily life? Is it tangential or is it central?

Well, let's see.

We accept of course wholeheartedly that we have an impact on our environment in various ways, both constructive and destructive just through the business of living. We create waste, for example, and atmospheric pollution as we heat our houses and drive a car or fly in an airplane. And we are only too well aware that the more of us there are, and the more we do those sorts of things, then the bigger is the impact on the environment.

Conversely, we also know that our environment clearly has an impact upon us, albeit in a slightly different way, in the sense that if we get up on a gray and rain-soaked Monday morning with the clouds scudding across the roof tops and the rain belting down, we might feel somewhat down in the dumps as a result. It gets to us. In the same way, we find it depressing to walk down a litter-filled city street, or when we see graffiti scrawled across a wall. Just as we can be uplifted by the sight of a cherry tree in full blossom, or the bright smile from the lady who is helping the morning school kids across the road. We fully accept that we interact with our environment in this sort of generalised, non-invasive way all the time.

The Buddhist principle of oneness of self and environment accepts all that, everything indeed that might be covered by that sort of everyday, piecemeal, somewhat superficial inter-action with bits of what goes on around us. But then it goes well beyond it. It declares that we *create* our own environment in the sense that it is essentially inseparable from our subjec-tive life state; the environment in which we find ourselves is an accurate reflection of our *inner* life state at that time.

That is a truly astounding idea. It posits that the strict di-viding line that we see so clearly between us and the vari-ous categories of matter that make up our environment, is an illusion, coming from our limited and partial vision. The reality, Buddhism declares, is that humans, animals, plants, the earth indeed, are part and parcel of the same entity, or the same continuum. Not separate and distinct, but inti-mately interconnected. And the bit that is the most difficult to accept is undoubtedly the animate and the inanimate connection. I don't think we should be overly concerned about finding such an idea *difficult* to come to terms with. It is as I've said, a huge and unusual concept.

Does science have anything to say that might help us to embrace it?

The Scientific Perspective

The late Richard Feynman was one of the most brilliant and influential theoretical physicists of the 20th Century. He was an astoundingly entertaining and illuminating lecturer on complex scientific issues, and in one of the collections of his brilliant lectures, he has this to say about the nature of matter, all matter.

"First of all there is matter, and, remarkably enough, all matter is the same. The matter of which the stars are made is known to be the same as the matter on earth...there are the same kinds of atoms there as on the earth. The same kinds of atoms appear to be in living creatures as in non- living creatures; frogs are made of the same 'goup' as rocks, only in different arrangements. So that makes our problem simpler; we have nothing but atoms, all the same, everywhere.'*

That is a radical, modern theoretical physicist coming surprisingly close, to one of Nichiren's most passionate declarations made some 700 years earlier,

"Life at each moment encompasses the body and mind and the self and environment of all sentient beings in the Ten Worlds as well as all insentient beings in the three thousand realms, including plants, sky, earth, and even the minutest particles of dust. Life at each moment permeates the entire realm of phenomena and is revealed in all phenomena.'

There it is, the clearest statement of oneness of self and environment,

"...life at each moment encompasses the body and mind and self and environment...."

So it is clearly not something that we can fudge.

But what about the second half of this issue that we are considering, the question of what might be called the *inter-action* between mind and matter, the nature of our interaction as living beings with the matter that makes up our environment? Do we just observe it, or do we have a much more involved and dynamic interaction with it? Once again I found it helped somewhat to turn to science, although, as I've already said, in no way do I believe that Buddhism needs science to validate its insights, and conversely, science doesn't extend its remit into the world of religion.

Einstein was somewhat unusual among scientists when he uttered his famous dictum, *"Science without religion is lame, religion without science is blind."*

That statement represents perhaps one of the most concise and powerful expressions of the fact that, to have the most satisfying understanding of the world and indeed the universe we inhabit, we need contributions from both. Science has very little if anything to say about the vast areas of human existence that lie beyond what can be seen and measured. Religion has a great deal to learn about the workings of the universe from the insights that science can provide.

Professor Arnold Toynbee adds a compelling viewpoint in Choose Life,

'Religion offers human beings a chart of the mysterious world in which we awoke to consciousness and in which we have to pass our lives. Although this chart is conjectural, we cannot do without it. It is the necessity of life. It is of far greater practical impor-

tance for us than most of science's tested and certified surveys of the tiny fraction of the universe that is accessible to us for scientific observation.'

On the question of interaction then, there is a fascinating story to be told. It represents something of a diversion on this personal journey, but I believe it will be worth it. It starts in the early decades of the 20th Century and since it represents a genuine revolution in our understanding of how matter is built up, the basic building blocks you might say from which everything in existence is made, including ourselves, it should cast light on how there might be genuine interaction between ourselves and our environment.

Very briefly, at the beginning of that period, scientists, physicists in particular, believed that they had a virtually complete picture of the way the world worked. There were just one or two minor pieces of the jigsaw to fill in, and they were confident that those missing pieces would be satisfactorily worked out within a couple of years or so, without any major surprises. They believed they were very close to what they liked to call a 'theory of everything,' a theory that comprehensively embraced all the particles and all the forces at work in the universe. Then, quite suddenly, within the space of a few years, the comfortable, cosy, established view of what the stuff of the universe is really like was utterly dismantled, never to be the same again. First, a brilliant young scientist called Rutherford at Manchester, proved that the atom, thought then to be the smallest particle, and thus the primary building block of the entire physical world we live in, wasn't in fact solid at all.

It wasn't, as had been believed, a bit like a microscopic melon with more solid bits scattered around inside it. It was, Rutherford was able to show, mainly *nothing*, mainly empty space that is, with a tiny solid nucleus at its centre and a variable number of smaller particles called electrons buzzing round it in various orbits. To get some idea of just how much space there is in what we confidently sit on as solid matter, the nucleus in the atom is about equivalent to a grain of sand stuck in the middle of a large football stadium. The electrons buzz round roughly where the stands are. I mention that not only because it's fascinating, but because it helps to show us just how partial and incomplete our common sense, down-to-earth view of the matter part of this proposition is.

Over the next few years a number of scientists in various parts of Europe began to explore this wholly new and unexpected microscopic universe that had suddenly been opened up to them. In terms of its impact on science it was a genuine revolution. It was rather like one of those ancient medieval maps which show just the outline of some newly discovered continent, with a vast empty space in the middle of it, with the words *here be monsters* written across it. Nobody knew what to expect next.

We are fortunate that the scientists who became the pioneer explorers in this strange new land were some of the most brilliant individuals the world has ever known, men like Albert Einstein and Niels Bohr and Werner Heisenberg and others. But even so, they were taken completely by surprise. Matter at this level, down below the scale of the atom seemed literally to have a mind of its own. It didn't follow any of the rules that had been so carefully built up over 300 years of science to describe the world that we can all see. They and their successors found literally dozens of new and hitherto unknown particles that fizzed into existence out of 'nothing,' and then disappeared again, back into nothing, seemingly at random.

They couldn't really comprehend what was happening. All they could hope to do was to find mathematical equations that could tell them how electrons might behave in different circumstances. That in effect, with brilliant imagination and insight, is what the scientists did. Those equations have been the basis on which, for example, the entire modern computer and electronic industries have been built ever since. The wonderful world of computation, and of global communications at the speed of light, on which all modern societies utterly depend, exists because those equations work, although scientists still don't fully understand the reality they describe. There is truly more in heaven and earth than is dreamed of in their equations! The debate continues over the extraordinary, Alice in Wonderland nature of this sub-atomic World, which became known as quantum mechanics.

Richard Feynman, with his rapier-like mind describes for us the heart of the problem;

*"...the difficulty really is psychological and exists in the perpetual torment that results from your saying to yourself," But how can it be like that?"which is a reflection of the uncontrolled but utterly vain desire to see it in terms of something familiar....I think I can safely say that no one understands quantum mechanics."**

But back to Buddhism, because the sole reason for this digression into one of the most extraordinary, and continuing, revolutions in the whole history of modern science, is to draw out two threads that seem to me to be really helpful in illuminating some of the fundamental things that Nichiren is trying to tell us, about the oneness of self and environment.

One is that we should remember that we are not talking here about some minute, insignificant, esoteric particles that exist somewhere out on the margins of our life. We are talking about the very basic building blocks of matter, out of which *all* things are made, without exception. Us, and our environment, in its entirety. Every galaxy, every plant and every animal, every human being. These particles are not earthbound. They exist throughout all matter in the universe. Thus the way they behave explains for example how photosynthesis works throughout the plant world to produce the food that all life depends upon; how the eye and vision work in all animals including us, and how the nuclear processes that go on inside the Sun produce the energy that is the basis of all life. So we are looking at a truly universal phenomenon, and all these seemingly separate processes are part of a whole.

The second point is no less important and no less surprising. The research carried out on these basic particles of all matter, carried out time and time again, over many decades by many different scientists, reveals one of the most extraordinary and still inexplicable effects in all of science, namely a profound interaction between the *mind* of the observer and the *matter* he or she is observing. The presence of the scientist, the very process of his being in the experiment, seems to alter the results. However carefully the scientists set up their experiments, however much they refine their measurements, the more they try to observe the behaviour of these basic particles, the more they realize that the process of watching itself changes the behaviour of the particles, in ways that still cannot be either fully explained or understood. It is almost as if the particles are aware that they are being observed. Scientists will no doubt berate me for using that anthropomorphic word *'aware'* but it makes the point.

Jacob Bronowski, the inspirational scientist and writer, described this new, strangely interactive, vision of the world revealed by these particles as follows,

*"The world is not a fixed, solid array of objects, out there, for it cannot be fully separated from our perception of it. It shifts under our gaze, it interacts with us, and the knowledge that it yields has to be interpreted by us."**

'It interacts with us' is indeed a startling claim, and one that comes very close to the idea we are exploring, the oneness of self and environment

Richard Feynman, again, in his characteristically casual style, describes the effect this strange interaction can have on the minds of scientists, when they seek to observe the behaviour of these sub-atomic particles,

"I am going to tell you what nature behaves like. If you will simply admit that maybe she does behave like this, you will find her a delightful, entrancing thing. Do not keep saying to yourself if you can possibly avoid it,"But how can it be like that?"because you will get into a blind alley from which nobody has yet escaped. Nobody knows how it can be like that!"

This has been a somewhat longer detour than I had intended, but I hope its purpose has been achieved. There is it would seem, however surprising that may be, a physical reality, observed by scientists in a multitude of experiments, that comes very close indeed to the powerful Buddhist declaration on the essential oneness of self and environment. Science uses words like 'interaction,' Buddhism uses the wonderfully expressive phrase, once heard never forgotten, 'two but not two.' They are not of course inter-

changeable, but they do seem to run in closely parallel
tracks.

But don't ask me how Nichiren, and those who came before
him, perceived and understood that essential truth long
before something close to it became apparent to quantum
physicists. I don't know that there is any answer to that
question.

But What Difference Does it Make?
But what about the implications, of the Buddhist view of the
oneness of self and environment? What difference does it
make in practical terms, for the way we see our lives? Well, it
is uncompromising. Put simply it declares that, at any particular time, the environment in which we find our self is a
reflection of our subjective life state at that time. If we are in
an angry, destructive, aggressive frame of mind, that will be
reflected back at us from the reactions of those around us,
and from the situations that arise. If on the other hand our
life state is high and our approach is consistently optimistic
and value creating, then that will flow out into our environment and have a profound influence on everyone we
encounter and the way the situations around us evolve. I
believe that claim, huge as it is, fits in with most people's
experience. We are aware that both pessimism and optimism
are highly infectious. We all prefer to live our lives
surrounded by positive, optimistic people. We all find that
our energies are sapped, by being amongst those who are
persistently pessimistic.

But that's a relationship between *people*, well within our daily
experience. The extension of this principle, to encompass an
interaction between our inner life state and our *physical* or
universal environment is undoubtedly much more difficult

to understand and accept. Hence the resort to the theoretical physicists, and the comforting knowledge that they are aware of it, even if they don't fully understand it either!

This altogether wider interaction is often described, rather grandly, as "putting ourselves in harmony with the universe." No one would deny that that is a fine phrase with tremendous resonance, albeit somewhat difficult to comprehend in its entirety? Yes, of course. But just as scientists can use the equations of quantum physics to bring us huge *practical* benefits, without fully understanding what is going on, so Nichiren tells us, we can gain huge practical benefits from this practice, without anything like a complete theoretical understanding.

Nichiren doesn't brush aside the difficulty. He understands our predicament completely. He goes out of his way to make clear that it is not necessary to have a complete understanding of the theory that underlies the teaching for us to put it to work in our lives and to benefit from it.

"Even though one neither reads nor studies the sutra, (The Lotus Sutra) chanting the title alone is a source of tremendous good fortune. The sutra teaches that...all the beings of the ten worlds, can attain Buddhahood in their present form. This is an incomparably greater wonder than fire being produced by a stone taken from the bottom of a river, or a lantern lighting up a place that has been dark for a hundred, a thousand, or ten thousand years."

There are countless analogies of course that we can draw from modern life, to illustrate that benefits aren't necessarily dependent upon our understanding of *how* systems work. They are not so poetic perhaps as those cited by Nichiren, but nonetheless useful to illustrate the point. We don't for example have to understand the complexities of the Otto four-stroke cycle to benefit from the fact that when we turn the ignition key the engine fires to enable us to set out on our car journey to pick up the children from school. Nor do we have to understand in the slightest the complex network of servers and routers and cables that enable us to send, at the click of a mouse and at the speed of light, a simple message of love and goodwill, from almost anywhere in the world to almost anywhere else. The immense complexity is reduced for our benefit to an extremely simple set of procedures. In the same way, we don't have to understand the complex biological and chemical pathways involved, to benefit from the little tablet we take with a dash of water three times daily after meals. We simply have to follow the prescription.

Nichiren is asking no more. In this sense then we might say that in following the Buddhist practice that he prescribes we are benefiting from the remarkable evolution of Buddhist thinking over some two and half thousand years, on the essential nature of human life. We don't have to know or to understand the complexities of that evolutionary process, in order to experience the benefits of the practice flowing into our lives, and being reflected in our environment. We simply have to follow the prescription.

The Wider Horizon

The Buddhist argument is that this principal of oneness of self and environment holds good even when it is scaled up to the level of society and beyond, to the society of nations. Although at first glance that might seem somewhat difficult to accept, there are plenty of examples from recent history, to illustrate this idea, that a nation will find reflected back from it's environment the aggression, for example, that it projects.

The past 100 years has been bedevilled by just such a situation. The 20th century has been described as the bloodiest in human history as the cycles of aggression and revenge between nations have been reflected back time and time again. Over 70 million people have been killed in wars of one kind or another, estimated to be more than in all previous centuries put together. Despite the world wide suffering and destruction, it is quite clear that history, in the sense of human experience, has provided us with precious few strategies to break this cycle. Certainly not diplomacy, and sadly it seems, not the United Nations, at least not yet. There have been some 200 armed conflicts since the last great global conflagration, and today the world bristles with more, and vastly more powerful, death-dealing weapons than ever before.

If you add to this situation the phenomenon of 24 hour news which wakes us up and puts us to bed with stories of death and disaster from one corner of the globe or another, and you have the perfect recipe for the sense of powerlessness that can infect the lives of many who are the slightest bit concerned about the problems facing a turbulent world. We can grieve in sympathy, or give a few pounds to this charity or that relief organisation, as the news of another disaster breaks, but what else can we do?

It might seem somewhat extreme to suggest that Buddhism can offer a strategy for tackling these widespread and seemingly insuperable problems, but that is precisely the promise that Buddhism holds out. It is the positive, hope-filled, value creating *something else* that we *can* do, and it represents in a very real sense the ultimate goal of Buddhist practice.

It all starts with the individual, with individuals determining to take responsibility for their own lives and gradually developing the courage and the optimism, the wisdom and the compassion to transform not simply their own lives, but the lives of those around them. As Daisaku Ikeda once again reminds us, with absolute clarity of vision.

"No one is born hating others."

The vision is one of growing numbers of people seizing the opportunity to create this transformation in their own lives, not simply for their own sake but for the sake of their families and friends, and all those in the wider circles of their life. Then indeed we could see a fundamental change in the way groups and societies and nations function. It is, we fully acknowledge, a great journey, and its distant objective is immense, nothing less than peace and harmony in our world.

But the Buddhist argument is that it is not a journey that is in any way remote or inaccessible. It starts right here.

CHAPTER TEN

The Challenge Of Change

We practice to shift our life from the lower worlds with their powerfully negative effects on our attitudes and behaviour, towards the higher life states of Learning and Realization, Boddhisattva and Buddhahood. As we do that, as we seek to move our whole life towards the positive end of the spectrum, so the promise is that we are also changing our environment. As *we* change, as we move away from anger say, with its basic concentration on our own ego, towards a more compassionate and responsive approach to others, so we find those qualities are increasingly reflected back to us from our environment. The challenges and the problems are no less frequent or severe, indeed they may well increase. The fundamental difference lies in the *clarity* with which we perceive them, and the strengthened ability to respond to them.

Clarity is an important factor. Nichiren describes one of the main benefits of the practice as being the greater clarity of vision that it brings; what he describes as a "purification of the senses." We see opportunities for example that we might not otherwise have noticed, or see problems arising at an earlier stage, when they can be more easily resolved. People who practice talk frequently about things seeming to run much more smoothly for them, or about happening to be in the right place at the right time, or about a fortuitous meeting that just happened to present a completely unexpected opportunity. We are told that there are no coincidences in Buddhism. The apparent smoothness, and the apparently fortuitous events are happening because we are seeing things more clearly, and responding to them more positively.

There can be a profound change too in terms of hopes and ambitions and expectations, what we are prepared to demand from our lives. It is frequently the case for example, that we have allowed ourselves to come to terms with a situation or a set of circumstances, despite the fact that, deep within us, we know the situation is unsatisfactory, or even the cause of a great deal of unhappiness in our lives. It might be a job that provides no opportunity for advancement, or a relationship that we have neglected, or a family situation that has become filled with anger. Through fear or apathy, or lack of courage, or simply because we have no idea how to initiate a change, without causing a rupture, we swallow it, we learn to live with those sorts of situations dominating much of our lives, often for year after year.

As we all know, few things are quite as difficult as effecting genuine change in our behaviour or attitudes. It has taken our lifetime to build them up, so it takes real energy and determination to set out to change them. They are all that we know. Perhaps above all, we need hope, a real sense that things *can* be changed.

One of the statements most commonly made about this practice, and one that embedded itself in my mind very early on after I started chanting, is that when you are faced with a difficult situation, and have no idea where to turn, when you start to chant about it, *"as if out of nowhere, comes hope."*

But of course it isn't from nowhere, it is from within, and it is the initial spark that is needed to ignite the process of change in a difficult situation. The hope may give rise to anger that you have allowed the situation to persist for so long, or it may inspire the inner resolution to do something about it. But however it expresses itself, it means that the process of change has already started. It may well be that the knowledge that some action has to be taken to change things, has lain dormant within your life for a long time, but the fear of change has been too great, or the circumstances have never seemed quite right. We are all very skilled at procrastination, at convincing ourselves that now isn't the best moment to face up to some difficult challenge. But as you continue to chant about the situation, not necessarily with any profound conviction, or with any clear idea of just *how* you might be able to resolve it, out of nowhere comes the hope, and the courage to tackle it. Buddhists will talk frequently of how, after months or even years of haziness, suddenly they become clear about what action needs to be taken, and of being able to face up to the task of initiating that action.

We might well have to take tough decisions that will disturb other people's lives, in challenging aspects of a relationship for example. Buddhism does not teach that we should not take that action because it disturbs or challenges other people, only that we should take it with compassion for the other person's needs, and accepting full responsibility for the causes we are making.

The time frame in which these changes take place   in our life and in our environment will of course vary immensely, since our circumstances and our environment are unique. It will also vary in relation to the commitment and sincerity of the practice. The fundamental promise of Nichiren Buddhism is that the benefits *will* begin to emerge, the changes *will begin to* take place as soon as we begin to chant. There isn't some sort of preliminary qualifying period. We don't have to build up a balance at the bank so to speak.

That's all very well, I can hear you say, for those who are lucky enough to believe in the practice, but what about those who have doubts? There are many Buddhist commentaries that tell us that we should never have doubts. I don't personally see how that is possible. Doubts are a normal part of all our lives, just as negativity is inherent in all our lives. Although it is important to be aware that they are not quite the same thing. Doubts breed caution, and there is nothing wrong with a bit of caution in a dangerous world. We might want to call it prudence, if that were not such an un-cool word these days!

Negativity however can disarm us, or render us immobile. It might tell us for example that Buddhist practice may well be able to deal with *other* peoples problems, but not *this* one, not the one that happens to be bugging *us*, because it is special, or deep-rooted, or because it has been part of our lives for so long, or because it involves a particularly intractable relationship, or whatever. Our own problems always seem to have a uniquely difficult twist to them. There is never any shortage of costumes for us to dress our negativity in, our evil twin is a master of disguise.

In other words, we have to learn to walk the tight rope between prudent caution, and disabling negativity. That negativity will always be there. Hear it, see it for what it is, but, Nichiren encourages us, don't give in to it. The act of recognition alone helps us to challenge it, and every time we do so, the more we come to believe in our ability to overcome it. Time and time again we return to this basic premise, Buddhism is not a soft touch. Life is tough, and what we are trying to achieve requires real effort and application. What we are trying to do is to get better at seeing problems for what they are, generating the courage to face up to them, and the perseverance to turn them round.

What do we Mean by Benefits?

In taking up this practice we are being invited to take part in an experiment. We are the focus of the experiment and our life is the test bed. Practice, we are told, without being grudging or half-hearted about it, give it a fair and genuine trial, and look for the benefits in our life. And that word *benefits* is almost a technical term in Nichiren Buddhism. It carries with it a very special set of meanings.

It might seem somewhat strange to be talking about the benefits of practising a religion at all, since that is not an idea that we are accustomed to apply to religious belief. We don't talk for example about the *benefits* of being a Christian, or not in my experience anyway. In general we think in terms of religions being principally a question of belief. We either believe in the view of life they present, or we don't. The idea of benefits doesn't really enter into it. So that can raise a problem when you first encounter Buddhism. It certainly did with me, since on the face of it, practising a religion in the expectation of benefits of whatever kind, in this lifetime, inevitably seems somewhat self-serving.

It is important however, to bear in mind a crucial distinction that has been touched upon to some extent in an earlier chapter. Most other major world religions are god-given, and are therefore essentially about the nature of the relationship between an individual and his or her creator. Buddhism by contrast is man-made, and it is concerned essentially with an individual's relationship with *himself*, and the rest of humanity. Its ultimate purpose therefore, is to enable ordinary human beings to realize to the full, their own unique potential, so that they are enabled to create the greatest possible value in any situation-for themselves and others. That is the key issue.

It is in that sense that the concept of benefits arises. You might say in fact, that the *whole* purpose of the practice, is about benefits, in this life, in the here and now. It is not in any way esoteric or other worldly. It is immensely practical and down to earth. It is not about some reward, some paradise, in an after life, it is about greater happiness, amidst the often harsh realities of ordinary daily life. The basic premise is that, whatever the life state of the person who takes up the practice, and however harsh his or her particular reality, these benefits are available to all.

So in that context, let's look at what this idea means in practice. Benefits are described as being experienced in two forms, inconspicuous and conspicuous.

Inconspicuous benefits, as the name suggests are changes that might occur within the spiritual or the unseen part of our lives. They may also occur relatively slowly, over many months. It's a bit like walking slowly up a hill, you don't realize quite how high you've climbed until you turn and look back down at the way you've come. In the same way, it may be that only when you look back over the months or the years, that you realize the extent of the changes that have taken place. Anxieties that you may have had all your life for example, no longer weigh so heavily.

People gain control of corrosive anger or cynicism for example that may have caused great damage to themselves and their relationships. Or they become able to combat depression more effectively, or find that they have much more self confidence in personal relationships. I have seen many people who have just started to practice, begin to tackle problems in their relationships that they simply haven't had the courage to confront for years. Others blossom in a matter of a few months and go from being somewhat withdrawn and diffident in public situations, to having the self confidence to debate and discuss complex issues freely in an open forum.

As you might expect inconspicuous benefits are very personal and unique to our own character and circumstances. But as you can also tell from the brief sketches above, they are of profound significance when we think of the sum total of pleasure and joy we have in life.

It may sound somewhat superficial, and indeed it may well be, although it is none the less true, to say that one of the things that struck me most when I first ventured into Buddhist meetings, was just how much people smiled and laughed, even when I happened to know that several among them were facing quite difficult challenges in their personal circumstances. Moreover people always seemed to have the energy and the vitality to support one another with tremendous warmth and sincerity. I am not saying of course that this circumstance is unique to Buddhism, only that it is a notable feature of Buddhist groups when they get together at regular discussion meetings and other events. There is a very strong awareness of the value of mutual support, and it is worth spending a moment or two to examine the implications of that, since it is wholly relevant to this issue of inconspicuous benefit.

Low Sense of Self Worth

However independently minded we may be, or think we are, we all need support. Isolation, the sense of being pretty much on your own, with no one to turn to for help or companionship, and a low sense of self worth are well documented, as being among the major causes of chronic depression. As it happens women are considerably more likely to experience the condition than men. I don't know that anyone has come up with a comprehensive thesis to explain this difference between the sexes, but one of the suggestions that has been put forward, is that even in this modern age of equality, women are still more likely to be at home than men, caring for children perhaps, and therefore more likely to feel caught up in a round of somewhat tedious repetitive tasks, day after day after day, from which they find it difficult to escape.

But it is a situation not necessarily linked to home life. A major study carried out recently in England for example, showed a similar effect among junior civil servants, people who tend to spend their working days carrying out a round of repetitive and uninspiring tasks. To the researcher's complete surprise, these lower level administrative staff, with generally very low levels of pressure or stress in their working day, were nonetheless far more likely to experience various forms of heart and arterial disease than their highly pressured, overloaded superiors. The underlying stress it was concluded, came not from overwork, but from the burden of routine and repetition, and the absence of challenge.

But the key point I wished to make is that although depression has been seen in the past largely as a psychological ailment, a matter of the mind so to speak, there is now very considerable research to show that severe depression can have a powerful effect on several major bodily systems such as heart rate and hormone levels and menstrual cycle, as well as being linked to a heightened risk of cardiovascular disease.*

If this is the case, it suggests that factors that would seem to be quite widespread in society, such as a low sense of self worth, or a prevailing feeling of isolation, or of having little control over one's daily life, are not simply the causes of a great deal of personal unhappiness. Their effect can be much broader and longer term. They can, it would seem, have a profound influence upon total bodily health, including the incidence of major life-shortening illnesses such as cancer and heart disease.

It is against this sort of background that we can begin to evaluate the truly beneficial effects of what are called *inconspicuous* benefits. Once again, I am not suggesting that these kinds of beneficial effects can *only* be achieved by Buddhist practice. There is considerable research to show that a religious dimension of whatever kind in one's life, can have a powerful, beneficial effect on general health. All I am saying is that there is not the slightest doubt that these kinds of beneficial, life-enhancing effects are experienced by many thousands, of people around the world, who have chosen to base their lives on the practice of Nichiren Buddhism.

Conspicuous Benefits

Conspicuous benefits, are, as the name suggests, far more apparent. They, relate to all the tangible, material elements that make up so much of the texture of our daily life. So conspicuous benefits might include such things as better living circumstances, a better house or a better job, a higher salary or a generally more favourable, more stable financial situation.

Nichiren Buddhism is quite clear on this point. It teaches that since we have both physical and spiritual needs, we must attend to both, if we are to achieve the most fulfilling and creative life of which we are capable. Buddhism is daily life, and *earthly desires* as they are called, needs or wishes that relate to the material aspect of our lives, are an integral and essential part of that life. Thus Nichiren Buddhism is not about *giving things up*. It argues that it is a perfectly normal and natural part of our humanity to desire a better home or a better paid or more satisfying job, or a more fulfilling relationship. So we shouldn't in any way try to reject these natural desires as being somehow unworthy of our spiritual self. Indeed the reverse is true. When we bring those life objectives into our practice and chant to achieve them, they can become the route to our human revolution, in the sense that whatever it is that stimulates us to chant, the very process of chanting begins to draw forth the courage and the life force and the compassion from within. The key thing is maintaining a balance.

As we have touched upon, the trouble arises, for us, and those around us, when Hunger becomes our dominant life condition. When the need for yet more possessions, yet more material benefits becomes the main motivational force in our life, and we pursue it, with little or no regard for the damage we do to our own values or what effect we might have on the lives of those around us. Buddhism is blunt about this kind of hunger. It describes greed as a poison in our system, indeed one of the three primary poisons that can infect our lives and become the source of immense and long-lasting pain and suffering. The other two are anger and foolishness. We all have them in our lives, to a greater or a lesser degree. The more these poisons exist in our own lives, the more we will see them reflected back into our lives from our environment.

Greedy people for example tend to see the whole world as being greedy. From that perspective they are simply doing what comes naturally. Angry people often wonder why *everyone* is so angry and bad tempered.

But let's stay with greed for a moment, because it has become so fashionable, if I may put it that way. It is of course the very basis of the great flood tide of consumerism that has swept us along and into record levels of personal debt and record levels of personal bankruptcies. But since the acquisition of a desired object is undeniably a pleasurable experience, why isn't more acquisition more pleasurable, and so on and on, to the realisation of ultimate happiness?

A recently published study in the City of London looked at people's attitude to their salaries. When people earned £60,000, and they were asked what salary they thought they would be *happy* with, it turned out to be over £100,000. Those who earned £100,000 thought they would be happy if only they earned around £250,000. Those who already earned £250,000 felt that they could really be *very happy* if they topped the million mark. Happiness it seems,, by the consumerist route, can always be just out of reach. A whole series of American studies into the nature of human happiness carried out in recent years, has delivered very similar results. Once basic needs have been met, it seems that additional income, even substantial amounts of it, did little or nothing to raise the sense of happiness or satisfaction with life. And more and more studies in this area tend to confirm its validity. However desirable wealth and possessions may seem, they are simply not enough.

The Buddhist teaching in this area is immensely realistic and down to earth. It argues that whatever delight may come from consumerism, it can only be short lived. It wears off as soon as the novelty of possession has worn off, and is replaced by the hunger for the next acquisition. By definition, a constant state of hunger can only lead to deep unhappiness. Essentially therefore Buddhism argues that the greatest joy in life comes from making and giving rather than taking; making and creating value that is, out of the here and now, out of our present circumstances, rather than being dependent upon what is in the showroom window.

In Tune with Modern Psychology

To approach this issue from a slightly different direction, it is fundamental to Buddhist teaching that the way we *look* at any situation or any environment is of the very greatest importance. That is to say, it is not so much the external circumstance that govern how it affects us, but how we *see* it. It is not so much what happens that causes us to suffer, as how we *respond* to what happens. Buddhism teaches therefore that as we develop and strengthen the inconspicuous benefits within our lives, the wisdom and courage and resilience, and the compassionate, positive outlook, so we develop the ability to transform any environment we find ourselves in.

Out of this we can create what the management gurus call a virtuous circle, a win-win situation. For as long as we are under stress in our own lives we don't really have much time and space for others. As we change, and develop the ability to handle our own situations with courage and resilience, so we have more resource left over so to speak, with which to support and encourage others. Moreover, we seem to find many more opportunities for doing so, from simply sharing experiences, to giving moral and emotional support, and devoting real time and energy to their problems. Giving and making, rather than taking and consuming. And Buddhism teaches paradoxically that exerting ourselves in this way, focusing outwards rather than inwards, concerning ourselves with the problems of others rather than concentrating solely on our own difficulties and concerns, is what leads to the most rapid growth in our own inner strength and resourcefulness.

Buddhism may have been promoting this idea for somewhat longer, but it is amply supported by the work of many modern psychologists.

Professor Richard Layard for example, in his book entitled *Happiness* makes it a central plank in his argument for a new moral code,

*"This should be the core of moral education, so that our children understand that what they give to life is more important than what they get from it. With that philosophy they will, in fact, remain happier, as modern psychology shows."**

Sonja Lyubomirski, research psychologist at UCLA is inclined to agree. As a result of her own and other research findings, she places acts of support to others very high on her list of actions that lead to greater level of individual satisfaction with life.

"Being kind to others, whether friends or strangers, triggers a cascade of positive effects. It makes you feel generous and capa-

*ble, gives you a greater sense of connection with others and wins you smiles, approval and reciprocated kindness."**

There are two key phrases there that relate directly to our argument, *"positive effects,"* and *"reciprocated kindness,"* since they both refer precisely to changes in the behaviour of others, changes that is to say in the environment, triggered by our behaviour.

We can accept quite readily, I think, that there is a constant interaction or interplay between ourselves and the society or the environment immediately around us, since most of us have direct experience of it. We can all recount instances where our anger or our joy has spilled over into those around us and sparked off an instant response. And we all know people who tend to carry their gloom and despondency, or their abundant optimism around with them like a suitcase, and spill it out into every room they walk into.

Fundamental changes in attitude and behaviour are, undoubtedly, extremely difficult to achieve. But as we change and develop spiritually, so we find that we have a greater capacity to see and understand other people's needs, or have greater resources of compassion to respond to other people's problems.

CHAPTER ELEVEN

A Long and Healthy Life.

Buddhism is very concerned with the issues of health and the pursuit of a long and active life. Just as we are responsible for all the causes we make, so we are responsible for taking the greatest care of our health, and doing all we can to develop our knowledge of what is and what is not likely to lead to a long and healthy life. Having the life brings with it the responsibility not to squander or waste it. We chant about it on a daily basis.

In one of the later chapters of the Lotus Sutra, Shakyamuni tells us a story about a wise physician and his many children. The doctor has to travel away for a while, and when he is away the children eat something that is obviously bad for them and they fall wretchedly ill. When he returns he finds them sick and ill and in great pain on the floor. The doctor immediately sees how far gone the children are and that he has no time to lose. He quickly diagnoses what is wrong with them and he prepares an appropriate medicine and tries to get them to take it. Some of the children immediately recognize that it is their father treating them and accept the medicine. The pain begins to subside and they begin to emerge from their illness. But some of the children are in so much pain that they don't recognize who the doctor is and refuse to take the medicine. They are in a dire straits, and it is only when at last they recognize precisely who this physician really is, and so take the medicine, that they too begin to come round, and emerge eventually from their pain and suffering.

This is of course a parable, and like most parables it works on many levels.

One of them undoubtedly is that the physician is to be seen as the Buddha himself, Shakyamuni, coming to the world with his great teaching of self-help. The many children are all ordinary human beings, us indeed, suffering in various ways from the three universal poisons of greed, anger and ignorance. The medicine that is offered is the Lotus Sutra itself. Those who are prepared to take the teaching into their life can overcome the sufferings that are inherent in human life.

At another level however this story can be seen as a Buddhist prescription for a long and healthy life. That is to say, it is not simply about overcoming the challenges and the problems that we encounter as a normal part of our everyday lives. It is also about applying the prescription, or the practice, in overcoming genuine illnesses of every kind, that afflict us from time to time, both in body and mind. From brief transient illnesses like colds and flu that might keep us in bed for a couple of days and make us feel a bit wretched, to longer term conditions that attack our whole way of life like depressions and phobias, right the way through to powerful, life–shortening illnesses like cancer and heart disease.

At the very core of the Buddhist view of healing lies the idea that we don't simply hand over responsibility for our health into the hands of medical professionals. We need both; the best medical knowledge that we can obtain, but always aided and abetted by our own natural, innate, self-healing powers.

Nichiren Buddhism teaches that chanting is in itself a powerful energising and revitalising process. It helps us to release the energy we need to challenge the negativity and the sense of defeat or personal frailty that often come with sickness, and replace them with hope and optimism. Hope is in itself a great healer. Without it there can be no determination to overcome the illness, and there is an ever- growing body of scientific and medical research to support and buttress the view that a strong and positive outlook is of immense importance both in resisting and in overcoming illnesses of every kind.

That is not to say that Buddhism in any way underestimates the powerful benefits of main stream medicine. Indeed the very reverse is true. It constantly advises its followers always to seek the very best medical advice and care available, but at the same time, in no way to underestimate the importance of the healing energy that can only come from within. We have the ability to strengthen and enhance our own natural immune response, and no medicine, however rare can replace that.

Just as Buddhism does not equate happiness with the absence of problems, so it does not equate good health with the absence of sickness. It goes further than that. It sees good health in the broadest sense as a state of life that is not simply free from physical or mental ailment, but one that is marked by vitality and energy and imbued with a sense of optimism and purpose. If we have that image in our minds we can see if we are selling ourselves short so to speak. If we settle for no more than a freedom from anxiety or worry, are we, we might ask ourselves, genuinely making the most of our lives? It is interesting that something very close to this idea has been adopted by the World Health Organisation in its definition of good health, where it talks of a state of physical, mental and social well being, rather than simply the absence of disease or infirmity.

But we have of course to be very cautious in this area. Doctors and scientists make it clear that it is very difficult indeed to set up anything approaching conclusive experiments to illustrate the precise correlation between psychology and disease, the relationship between how we are thinking and feeling, and the progress of an illness. But that having been said, there is a growing number of medical papers that seem to illustrate a connection between emotional states and certain illnesses; hope and optimism linked to good health and shorter healing periods, while prolonged anxiety and melancholy have been associated with life shortening illnesses such as cancer and heart disease.

Bearing both those views in mind, both the caution and the optimism, let us look just very briefly, at some accounts of people who have turned to their practice to challenge profound illnesses of many kinds. There are many stories available in various journals of people who have been through similar experiences. These are neither the most remarkable nor in any way the most dramatic. These are simply ordinary people who happen to practice in my particular corner of London.

The Story of Quitterie.
Quitterie is a young married woman in her late 20s. She has had a very ordinary life so far as health is concerned with no particularly outstanding illnesses or ailments. Shortly after the birth of her first child she encountered very severe stress

in that her baby son Kynu suffered from an unsteady and irregular heart beat. In his first year of life the condition became serious enough to require hospitalisation and an operation to fit a pacemaker. The little boy seemed to recover very rapidly and was soon developing normally, learning to crawl and then walk, and then being able to speak and go to play school with other little children of his own age. However there was, perhaps inevitably, that constant latent anxiety that her son might suffer some catastrophic reverse.

Despite her anxiety Quitterie seemed normal enough. There was no overt change in her appearance, but she began to feel increasing lethargy and weariness. Her body felt bruised and her legs ached. She went to see her doctor but he could find nothing specific that he could treat, apart from suggesting a healthy balanced diet and plenty of rest. But the condition got steadily worse. Within a matter of months she was barely able to get up and look after her child and completely unable to walk up and down stairs, because of the pains in her joints. She was sent for a series of urgent blood tests. Several anomalies emerged from the tests, but by far the most alarming was the state of her immune system. It was in a state of collapse. Her white blood cell count for example was down below the extreme danger level.

At about this time Quitterie had met someone who practised Nichiren Buddhism and she learned about chanting. When she realized just how ill she was, at first she simply panicked and had no idea what to do. Then she decided to "Give the chanting a chance," as she put it, "What had I to lose?"

So she determined to chant at least an hour a day, every day, come what may, concentrating on the idea of getting her white cell count back to normal.

Other members of the SGI learned about her situation and went round regularly to chant with her. One was a friend who had herself, only recently taken up the practice. Another was a lady who had a very strong practice indeed and who was prepared to give her time to help Quitterie through this crisis. The support was crucial. Quitterie found it very difficult to stick to her determination. Chanting was a wholly new experience, and keeping it going for around an hour a day required from her huge amounts of determination.

Two weeks or so later Quitterie was required to go back to the hospital for a check up. When the blood samples had been taken the doctor asked her what she was taking in addition to her medication. Somewhat puzzled Quitterie replied that she wasn't taking anything that she knew of. The doctor then asked her if she had changed anything about the way she lived. At first she couldn't think of anything, and then she said that she had taken up chanting every day. As Quitterie tells it, the young lady doctor rolled her eyes as if in disbelief and said something like "Oh really!" But she then said that *whatever* she was doing, she should continue to do it because her white blood cell count was much higher, still way below what it should be, but higher than the doctor could ever have believed possible in so short a time.

This was of course huge encouragement. Quitterie still found it immensely difficult to chant for an hour on a daily basis, even though she perceived that when she did so she felt strengthened, but she did what she felt able to do. A week or so later her white blood cell count was very much closer to normal levels, and Quitterie felt herself to be much stronger. She no longer spent most of the day in bed. She was able to summon up the strength to go shopping, and resume her studies, and take up the care of her son again during the day, and so on.

Both Quitterie and her husband now practice Nichiren Buddhism. They hold local meetings in their home and Quitterie has the energy and the vitality to welcome and look after everybody. She still gets attacks of fatigue and weariness however, and when she talks about them it is clear that she still finds it wholly surprising just how much she is helped out of these attacks, by increasing her chanting. Quite recently, for example, when Kynu, now a child of 3, went through major heart surgery to re-engineer his pacemaker, Quitterie, supported by a group of SGI friends, increased her daily chanting to carry her through the stressful period. She was undoubtedly frightened for her child but her general health didn't falter. Indeed she said that she felt so strengthened that she was able to re-main buoyant and positive and do what was most important to her, namely to provide most of the care and mothering, that Kynu needed, herself.

The Story of Jocelyn

Jocelyn is a young Chinese woman in her mid 30s. She is single, professionally trained, and she has a very busy and active life. She also has a very strong Buddhist practice, chanting at least an hour a day, reading and studying on a regular basis and getting fully involved in discussion groups and other activities with her Buddhist friends.

About a year or so ago Jocelyn began to experience pains in her abdomen. She had a series of tests but no specific cause was identified. However over the next few months the pains grew steadily worse, until, from time to time they prevented her from going to meetings. Eventually doctors identified the cause as a substantial growth in her uterus. It was found to be a non-malignant cyst, but her consultant wanted it to be removed as a matter of urgency.

Jocelyn however, wasn't sure what to do. She found it difficult to commit herself to having the operation, even though she was often in considerable pain. She decided to chant about the dilemma for some time, and then she took a remarkably courageous decision. She decided to try to overcome the cyst simply using her Buddhist practice, and her considerable knowledge of alternative remedies.

So that's what she did. She basically built her life for the time being, around the task of getting rid of the cyst, harnessing her strong belief in the beneficial effects of the practice. She made a determination that she would bear the pain, live her life as normally as possible in terms of work, but shape her life to achieve this goal that she had set herself. That meant for example that she got up earlier every morning so that she could chant a minimum of two hours a day, focusing strongly on the removal of the cyst and the healing of her body. I met Jocelyn many times during this period. She never once complained, even though it was quite clear that she was going through a considerable amount of pain, and she made a huge contribution to the various Buddhist activities that were going on. Indeed she rarely if ever talked about her troubles. It took two years of immense determination. But now, she has been assured by her consultant that the cyst has gone, along with the pain.

The Story of Margaret

Margaret is a writer, in her mid 50s. She lives alone now, although she has been married and has several children. She is by nature a very quiet and gentle person and carefully guards her privacy. She has never had any religious inclinations, but some years ago she felt strongly that she needed some supportive spiritual dimension in her life, and she tried a form of Buddhist meditation with some success. Some years ago she encountered Nichiren Buddhism and was attracted by what it seemed to promise. She tried chanting for a while but found that it didn't really work for her, and gave it up after a few months. But she was still looking for something that she felt was missing at the centre of her life, and after a gap of some months she came back to Nichiren Buddhism.

She went through what might be called an extended period of experimentation with chanting, and going to discussion meetings and talking to people. She wasn't in any hurry. Eventually she felt able to commit herself to the practice on a regular basis. One of the comments she made not long after that event is I think, well worth noting, She said"It somehow strengthens your spirit. You don't feel so scared of what life might bring."

Not very long after Margaret had committed to the practice she was dismayed to find that she had a well-defined lump in her breast. Margaret has had a deep fear of illness and of cancer in particular, for many years. Some twenty years earlier she had to undergo several quite difficult operations to remove benign lumps from near one breast.

The initial diagnosis was not hopeful. Doctors made it clear that they thought that they would have to operate quite quickly. However more extensive tests indicated to Margaret's profound relief, that though the lump was large, it was not in fact malignant. Despite that, the doctors advised that given her age and the size of the lump it would be prudent for it to be removed.

Margaret remember, was a young Buddhist, with less than a years committed and regular practice behind her. Indeed that is one of the reasons why it seems to me that this experience is so valuable.

With great courage, Margaret decided that she wasn't going to have the operation. She was going to put all her trust in the strength of the practice and she was going to "chant" the lump out of her life. She had been chanting strongly to get through the stress of the process of analysis and diagnosis. Now she allocated more time each day, two hours, three hours some-times, supported by a number of her relatively new SGI colleagues.

For a while there was no change, but Margaret had accepted that it wasn't going to be an easy process. Within less than a year however the lump began to diminish. Margaret went through several medical examinations, and steadily, the lump went away. Not only has it not re-appeared since, but Margaret's energy and vitality are markedly higher than they have been for several years.

Margaret is very reluctant to tell the story to others, but she has no doubt in her own mind that her sheer determination to be better, enabled her to rid herself of the unwelcome lump.

What Sort of Conclusions Might We Make?

There are many comments that might be made about these experiences, but two seem to me to be particularly important. As I have already mentioned, they were not in any way specially selected. They simply occurred in my own local area to people whom I knew personally. I know, as a matter of fact, rather than of supposition, that many people practising in other parts of the UK and elsewhere, have similar experiences to relate.

The second point is rather broader, and it is that although I am writing as a practising Buddhist, from a Buddhist perspective, I am not suggesting that helping oneself to heal in this way, brought about by a combination of strong practice and main stream medicine, is a Buddhist preserve. It is quite clear that self-healing has been recorded over many centuries, in many cultures and in many religious environments. Moreover a great deal of research has been carried out in recent years to explore the extent to which faith and prayer, of whatever kind, can have a beneficial effects upon rate of healing.

Dr Herbert Benson, for example, Professor of Medicine at Harvard University in Boston conducted a long series of clinical studies in the 1990's into the effectiveness of various forms of prayer and religious practice. The results of these studies are set out in his account *Timeless Healing: The Power and Biology of Belief*. His conclusion, essentially, is that many forms of repetitive prayer, arising from faith, can have powerful beneficial effects on critical physiological factors such as lower blood pressure, stable heart rates, and heightened immune systems.

That is to say, many kinds of prayer, used on a regular basis and, importantly, linked to a fundamental belief system, have been shown to help people to recover from their illness or their operation, more rapidly or more completely, often against difficult odds. Dr Benson coined a memorable phrase to define this healing process; he described it as returning to *"remembered wellness."*

From the multiplicity of studies of this nature in many parts of the world, it would seem that the power of faith and prayer in many forms, to revitalise and stimulate the effectiveness of the immune system is difficult to ignore. A positive approach to life, whatever its source, is health-giving, and Buddhism clearly recognizes the validity and the virtue of the world's rich diversity of spiritual and religious traditions, no one of which has a monopoly of the truth.

From the viewpoint of Nichiren Buddhism then, the process of chanting puts the control, or the choice back into our hands. Whatever the nature of the attack upon us, it enables us to shift our position from the negative to the positive; from being weighed down and in some measure diminished by the illness, to challenging it, to having hope and courage and confidence that we can overcome it, rather than relying solely on the efficacy of the medical treatment we are receiving.

The Concept of Visualisation

In his book entitled *Modern Buddhist Healing* Charles Atkins adds a slightly different but very illuminating perspective to the sorts of experiences that we have been talking about. He describes a form of therapy that involves chanting while focusing your thoughts on, or actually visualising, the particular parts of the body that you are deeply concerned about. As you do so, you imagine or visualise the body marshalling its healing forces and bringing them to bear on the affected area. It might for example be a broken arm that you are recovering from, or open-heart surgery, or a lump in the breast, or persistent headaches. But whatever the illness or the cause of suffering, it is essentially, a method that enables you to concentrate and focus your inner energies, like a laser you might say, onto the areas of the body where healing is most needed.

Charles Atkins has been a Nichiren Buddhist for over 30 years and he poured all his faith and energy into this method, which he calls *"mantra-powered visualisation,"* to help him overcome cancer, a life threatening attack of Hodgkin's Lymphoma, that he experienced when he was in his mid thirties. As he writes,

"For me mantra-powered visualisation was a powerful tool against illness, when I wasn't even strong enough to pick up a hammer. Words have power. Some might scoff at the ability of some strange sounding words to produce such exciting results. Just the phrases "I love you," or "I hate you," have a powerful effect on our psyche. It is imperative that we strengthen our ability to take firm control of our mind, through the determination of our spirit, especially when our body seems to be doing the opposite of what we consciously want it to. At the core of our being is a master physician, a "medicine king" if you will, who can quicken recovery with the help of your doctor."*

It is an approach that is very much in accord with the general principle that, in chanting about any problem we encounter in life, we should chant not about the problem, but about the *solution*. That may seem to be something of a quibble, but in fact it is crucial. If we chant about the problem itself we are in a sense pouring our energies into it, into the negative end of the equation, making it loom ever larger in our lives. Whereas as soon as we switch our attention to the *solution*, or to the kind of *outcome* we wish to see, we are immediately looking forward, to the resolution we wish to achieve, and energising all our spiritual resources in that direction. We are looking forward that is, rather than back.

One of the greatest qualities in Buddhism that makes it potentially such a power for good in our lives, is that it provides us with a clear philosophical framework for looking at everything that occurs to us, including sickness, in a positive light, as a powerful source of growth. However much a paradox that may seem, however difficult a challenge it may be initially, you can see that it is a continuously self-reinforcing process. The more you do it, the more you *can* do it. Thus the more we find it possible to see everything that happens to us, the knocks and the setbacks as well as the joys and successes, from this standpoint, the more our confidence grows. We develop what Daisaku Ikeda calls *"a fighting spirit."* We begin to see that we do indeed have within us this ability to transform everything, even the challenge of severe illness, into a source of growth. Central to that understanding is the Buddhist concept of the oneness of body and mind.

CHAPTER TWELVE

Oneness of Body and Mind

At the heart of the Buddhist view of a healthy life, lies the understanding that there is no fundamental distinction or separation between the physical aspects of our life and the spiritual. It uses the beautiful clarity of the phrase "two but not two," to describe this relationship. That is to say, the mind and the body may *appear* to be different entities. Indeed, in the West we are very much conditioned by the overwhelming cultural and medical tradition to view them in that way. But Buddhism teaches that that is an incomplete view of the reality. The fundamental reality, Buddhism argues, is that they are simply two different aspects of each individual life. They are inseparable, as distinct and yet as intimately related, as the two sides of a sheet of paper, or as your body and its image in the mirror. They are both separate and yet inseparable; one without the other is inconceivable, if you move one, you inevitably move the other. Whatever affects one will inevitably affect the other, and not simply at a superficial level, but down at the level of the basic life support systems in the body.

Reading Other People's Minds

My own view is that we know instinctively that this is the case, since we constantly use this moment-by-moment interaction between mind and body in the way we handle our relationships with other people. Body language for example is a crucial form of communication. As members of the human tribe we have become immensely skilled at reading all the *external* physical symbols of the face and body, to try to get a grip on what is going on in another person's *mind*. If you think about it, our ancestor's survival must often have depended on getting it right. If we feel intense anger for example, which exists as an emotion in our mind, it reveals itself in our body as a flushed face and staring eyes, a stiffening of all the facial muscles and often violent movements of the hands and arms. Moreover we now know that deep within the body whole systems are responding to that anger in the mind; hormones are setting the heart racing and the blood pounding, preparing the muscles for a fight. That is to say, the interaction between mind and body is both manifest, and complex and widespread throughout our entire being.

Today it may not be our survival that depends on an accurate reading of the mind through the signals transmitted by body, although it still has a key role to play. It may just be that we recognize that it's a good time to leave our boss's office, or to move out of our partner's missile range. But whatever it may be, we are responding to the intimate connection between the mind and the body, between the seen and the unseen. Conversely if we see someone perhaps with a slack demeanour, and lifeless eyes and an apparent absence of appetite for life, even if they are a total stranger, we know that we are looking at the outward and physical signs of deep anxiety or depression within. Indeed we now have the ability to look deeper within the body, where the eyes can't see, to discover that prolonged depression, can affect half a dozen vitally important physiological systems in the body, from heart rate and blood flow to sex hormone levels and the functioning of the entire immune system.*

Of course people can dissemble. In fact we are very good at that. We can deliberately transmit the outward and physical signals of anger or of affection, when we feel no such emotion, simply to lead other people astray. But that in a way simply serves to prove the point. The mind and the body are so intimately connected that we can even *manipulate* the connection, to serve our own ends. Indeed there is a school of anthropology that argues that the huge and still unexplained expansion in the size of the human forebrain was perhaps brought about by this very phenomenon, namely, the sheer complexity of human relationships.

We acquired this huge brain as recently as around 100,000 or so years ago, when human life was relatively simple; hunting animals, gathering berries and fruits, making relatively simple stone and wooden and bone implements. So, the fundamental, and still unresolved problem, is, what on earth was the trigger, the stimulus, that caused us to develop this huge brain long before we actually *needed* it, or could make use of it. It is the very same brain remember that is capable of calculating the movements of the stars, and defining the fundamental relationship between energy and matter throughout the entire Universe, and writing Hamlet, or the 5th Symphony, and putting a man on the moon, and creating the World Wide Web, etc etc. It remains a huge mystery.

One intriguing theory that has, I think, a great deal going for it, is that we needed this huge brain to cope with the sheer complexities of *human relationships.* As family and tribal groups became larger and more diverse, so, the theory goes, success and even survival, came to depend upon the skill with which anyone could handle the relationships with a wider range of other people, from quickly grasping their real motives, to manipulating their responses. The larger brain was needed, that is, to cope with the endless complexities and subtleties, of reading the *inner* motivations of others, from the *external* signals they were transmitting. Were they friendly or were they hostile? Were they true, or were they false? Those who were most skilled at it clearly had a better chance of survival. And so the big brain was handed down to us. It's a nice theory.

But whether it's true or false for those times, if we bring that stone age hypothesis up to date, it *is* very much part of our life today. If we think even for a moment about our circle of friends and colleagues, we are completely accustomed to making judgements not only about the inner character of those around us, but about subtle changes in their mood and motivation. How do we do it? By reading all the external physical manifestations, from facial expressions and gestures and body posture, through to the movement of the eyes and the level of the voice, and so on. Every hour of every day we exercise this skill, we seek to learn about what is going on in the mind and the spirit, as it is revealed in the body, because deep within us, we believe that the two are so intimately inter-linked.

There is one other example of this mind-body inseparability that appeals to me immensely, and which has even been given a scientific name. It is called the Biophilia Effect. It has been shown that the love of the natural world is so deeply embedded within our nature that when we walk in green fields or deep and shady woods, the pleasure we feel in our *spirit* is mirrored by a powerful and refreshing effect upon our physiology, in terms of reducing the blood pressure for example and even relaxing the facial muscles. We relax far more completely that is, when we are surrounded by greenery, than we do when we are surrounded by bricks and mortar. Physical exercise in an urban environment may burn as many calories and stretch as many muscles as running in the country, but only in the latter it seems, do we experience the added bonus of this mind-body interaction.

The Power of The Cultural Tradition

However much we may instinctively recognize and accept this mind-body interplay, we are all, to a greater or lesser extent, captives of our cultural and spiritual traditions. In the West over thousands of years, the mind and body have traditionally been regarded not only as entirely separate entities, but very often as entities in bitter conflict one with the other. This is particularly true in the Christian era, although this sort of dualism is not restricted to Christianity. There has, historically, been a deeply rooted tendency to see the mind as pointing upwards towards heaven, the godly part of us, reflecting our highest spiritual aspirations. Meanwhile the leaden body is bound to earth, the animal part of us, weighed down by its burden of earthly desires and animal-like instincts. Thus the spirit was, and to some extent still is, seen as the source of good to be encouraged, the body or the flesh, the source of evil to be subdued.

We can see this intense dualism, where the mind and the body are set apart and in conflict, expressed in various ways at various times in history. In Hinduism for example, with the practices of asceticism, the body has to be punished and denied virtually to the point of extinction, in order to liberate the spirit and enable it to move forward on its path towards enlightenment. In Medieval Europe, severely scourging the body for its sins with whips and thorns became a regular religious practice. My own family name is derived from a similar albeit somewhat milder practice. "Going woolward," was the term used to describe the wearing of a coarse woollen shirt close against the unprotected skin, to punish the flesh and to elevate the spirit of a friar who had broken his vows. The Inquisition went to the lengths of completely eliminating the corrupt bodies of its victims by burning them at the stake, as the only sure way of releasing their troubled spirits. In Cromwell's Puritan England rowdy physical pleasures such as maypole dancing and funfairs and theatre going were seen as giving in to the lowly and degrading demands of the body, and polluting the dignity and purity of the human spirit.

We may well regard all those measures, or most of them anyway, as being buried deep in the past, but the cultural tradition is a long one, and undoubtedly the memory lingers on. Even in modern times, many people who are not necessarily practising Catholics adopt the practice of giving up some *physical* pleasure, eating chocolate perhaps or drinking wine, during the period of Lent, as a symbolic physical "punishment" that is seen in some way to lighten or ease the path of the spirit.

But the point I really want to make is that, as a result of this long cultural tradition that persists in various ways into the modern era, not least in much of modern medicine, it may well be quite difficult for us to accept this profound idea that there is no fundamental distinction between our spiritual and physical selves, our mind and our body. After all we can see the body, but we can't see the mind. We certainly can't see that they are *"two but not two."* It is a concept therefore that we need to grapple with. A recognition that both suffering and happiness come from within, rather than without, is central to this practice of Buddhism. So too is an understanding that pre-eminent in our healing process is our own life force. Above all other factors, chanting can help us to maintain our good health, or to recover it. It is the most compelling concept in the Buddhist view of a healing.

Fortunately, we have today the growing body of scientific and medical evidence to help us in our understanding. Indeed I learn from my doctor sons that an increasing number of leading medical schools are taking this factor of self-healing into account; including in the curriculum of today's student doctors at least something about the profoundly beneficial healing effects of alternative or spiritual therapies that might well include such practices as meditation and prayer.

The Placebo Effect

Scientists and doctors have long known about the intimate mind-body interaction that goes on with the so-called "placebo effect." This is in fact a hugely important indicator of the power of two-but-not-two. So let me deal with it very briefly. In carrying out studies on the effects of new drugs there is a very clear test protocol whereby one group of patients will be given the actual drug, while another group, the "control group," as it's called, will be given an equivalent and look-alike dose of some totally inert substance, such as a sugar pill or some such concoction. The purpose of this method is, of course, to enable the doctor-scientists to see clearly the difference in the *effects* on two similar groups of people, between those who take the drug, and those who don't.

Of course, no deceit is involved. Everybody recruited into the test is aware of the arrangements. But in order for the test to be effective it is important that none of the *patients* knows which group he or she is in; who receives the active pill, and who receives the dummy, the *placebo* as its called. However it is now widely understood that many of the people who receive the *dummy* pill, will nevertheless, demonstrate *positive* effects, often to remarkable extent, as if they had in fact, been receiving the new medicine. That is to say, the mere *belief* that they have been receiving the medicine has had the same, or a very similar effect, as actually taking it. The power of the mind that is, has had a powerful physiological effect on the body.

Moreover there are a number of illnesses that, even in conventional medical terms, have long been regarded as arising largely from the state of mind of the patient, rather than from physical causes. Indeed these conditions have been specifically labelled as *"mind-body"* conditions, or "psychosomatic."Typical symptoms that are often described in this way are internal ulcers, and various painful skin conditions such as eczema and shingles. That is to say conventional medicine fully accepts that the chronic stress or anxiety in the *mind* of the individual, or perhaps the shock to the entire system occasioned by some distressing event, rather than any physical malfunction, can trigger a profound effect in the *body.*

That having been said, it is important to emphasis once again that Buddhism does not in any way teach that we can in some way *replace* modern medicine by the application of strong belief. Buddhism teaches that we need both. The wisdom to get the best analysis and treatment that modern medicine can provide, and the courage to recognize that what ultimately heals our mind and body is our own life force. We need both.

More recent research has demonstrated for example that even on a moment-to-moment basis, there is a direct link between our emotions, what we are feeling in our heads you might say, and the physical operation of the heart. During times of extreme mental stress and powerful negative emotions such as anger or sadness, the actual pumping effectiveness of the heart is reduced. When we are feeling positive emotions such as optimism or joy, or when patients are encouraged to concentrate on positive and constructive emotions, the heart is seen to be in its most responsive and flexible state.

In the longer term a continued negative life state is now clearly associated with a widespread deterioration in the body's systems. Different researchers highlight different physiological effects, but they include such life threatening conditions as a generally weakened immune response to disease, and increased risk of heart disease and strokes and increased risk of cancer.

Fortunately, the converse is also true. There is increasing evidence to show that a strongly optimistic and positive approach to life boosts the immune system and so enhances our ability to resist or overcome disease, to lower blood pressure and lead to more regulated heart rate. Happiness if you like, can make the heart beat longer.

If one looks at this growing body of medical and scientific research, from a Nichiren Buddhist standpoint, it would seem clear that this practice places an immensely powerful tool into our hands, since it gives us the ability to choose. Every day we can choose to challenge the negativity in our lives, which we now know, can have such harmful effects upon our physiological health. Every day we can shift our lives towards the positive end of the spectrum, which we now know brings so many healthful benefits. It is clear that good health is not simply the absence of sickness or anxieties at any particular point in time, it is rather the creation of a strong and positive life state, that we can choose to strengthen each day, which enables us to challenge and overcome the sickness and the anxiety that will, inevitably, come into our life, rather than be cast down by it.

Coming Home

As you might expect there are just about as many reactions to this practice as there are people who encounter it. Everybody has a personal view, but one view that is very often expressed, albeit in somewhat different terms, is, "somehow it's like coming home." Extraordinarily, something similar to it was often expressed in Shakyamuni's time. Many of his early followers are reported to have said that it was like joining the stream.

On its own that is not enough. Nichiren's teachings need to be discussed and chewed over and tested out against the reality of our own lives, as indeed, he requires us to do. He constantly tells us to take nothing at face value, but to look for actual proof of the practice in the day-to-day movement of our lives and relationships.

But neither of course should that initial reaction of the spirit simply be cast aside. This Buddhism is not about the intellect, or rather, not solely about the intellect, it is very much about the heart. That is particularly important in relation to these two fundamental principles; the oneness of self and environment we were discussing in an earlier chapter, and in this one, the oneness of body and mind. Both of them are undoubtedly challenging ideas. In many ways they run counter to the cultural and spiritual tradition many of us have grown up in. But it is important that we see them for what they are, because these are not in any way just a clutch of interesting, but somewhat remote and academic theories. They are above all, a practical description, of our daily reality.

These two fundamental ideas, taken together, seek to explain how it is that the practice of chanting can have such a profound effect on our own lives, and on our environment. As *we* change and create value within our lives so we send the ripples of change out into our environment. Similarly, because the mind and the body are not separate but simply two intimately related aspects of our individual life, chanting brings mind and body into harmony, and in so doing, it releases the spiritual energy that gives us the vitality to help heal our body or lift ourselves out of despair.

CHAPTER THIRTEEN

Modern Views of Life and Death

It is impossible to write a book on Buddhism without at
least touching on the issue of rebirth or reincarnation.
Partly because it is one of the few Buddhist terms that can
be said to have become common currency in the West. Indeed it is often the first issue that people will raise when
they learn that you are a practising Buddhist because they
find it so intriguing.

But there is, I would argue, another and far more important
reason for talking about the Buddhist view of what happens
at the end of this particular life, and that is simply that it is
immensely positive. It has the potential to be immensely
beneficial in all sorts of ways. To those who shy away from
any consideration of death whatsoever, and who simply refuse to come to terms with it, as well as to those who carry
around a considerable burden of fear and anxiety about it. I
came to Buddhism from Catholicism. I had great difficulty
with the idea of rebirth or reincarnation for a long time. To
be absolutely frank, I still do. But on the basis of that experience I would go so far as to argue that whatever one's belief,
or absence of belief, some study of the Buddhist view of
death, and how death relates to life is both illuminating and
helpful. At the same time it is important to say that it is not

necessary to comprehend or to believe in the idea of reincarnation to take up a Buddhist practice, not at all.

The basic fact that we all have to face up to of course is that
all life, ultimately, is about death. There is an old Hindu
legend to the effect that a god once posed the question,
"What is the greatest mystery in the Universe?" No one would
dare to answer. No on wanted to hazard a response to so
profound a question. After a long pause the god provided
the answer himself.

*"The greatest mystery is the fact that although every human being
who has ever lived on the planet has died, no individual human
being alive today finds it easy to understand that this will happen
to him too."*

Shakyamuni tells us a similar story. In one village he visited
we are told, he was approached by a mother, stricken with
grief at the death of her child. She implored him from the
depths of her agony to use all the powers at his disposal to
revive her dead child. Shakyamuni did not rebuff her. Instead
he said he would revive her child, if only she would go round
the village and bring him back a simple mustard seed from a
house where the family had never lost anyone to death. The
lady went weeping from house to house, seeking her mustard
seed from the house where no one had died. As she did so,
she slowly came to the acceptance of the inevitability of
death, for all living things.

These stories strike the target precisely. They are truly unfor-
gettable. We all immediately recognize the truth that lies at
their heart. The extraordinary fact is that, as far as science can
tell us, man is the only form of life in the universe that is
aware of its own mortality. Everything in the universe, non-

living as well as living, goes through the same cycle, the grand cycle of birth, growth, decline and death. All the evidence we have indicates that this never-ending cycle applies to everything that we know about, from the mightiest galaxy spinning in its panoply of light on the dark edge of the universe, to the smallest microbe emerging in the darkness from under some speck of soil.

I will come back to that thought, since it is quite important in the Buddhist view of life and death, but the particular point I am concerned with now is that only human beings are aware of the inevitability of death from an early age. All other creatures die of course, but as far as we know they only become aware of their death if at all, briefly before it occurs. So in one sense we can say that we occupy a very privileged position. In another we might say that we carry a great burden, in that we can contemplate death from afar off, and think about what it means in relation to life. Indeed, it has been said many times that the mystery of death is the greatest problem facing each individual.

For most of us the burden seems to weigh far more heavily than the privilege. However natural and normal and everyday an event death may be, it's not a subject we want to spend any time thinking about. Indeed we go to very great lengths to avoid it. It may be thrust under our noses virtually every day of the year through newspapers and television reports of accidents close to home and disasters further afield, in one corner of the world or another.

But that is definitely not the same as contemplating death on an individual level. In fact despite the progressive sophistication and liberalization of western society, death is still pretty much a taboo subject. When did you last spend even a few minutes discussing it? Throughout the West in particular we have gone to very great lengths to insulate ourselves from it by ensuring that dead people are "dealt with" by a small number of specialised medical and social groups, doctors and nurses and morticians and so on. So successful have we become in fact over the past few decades, that although many thousands of people die one way or another every single day, most people in the West can still go through life without having any contact with death whatsoever, until perhaps a close relative passes away, or indeed until they face their own demise.

That is, if you think about it, an extraordinary situation. But many people would argue I'm sure, that that is pretty much as it should be, that the balance is about right. Life is about life, it is full of light and variety and opportunity. Whereas death is about a dark and mysterious void into which we must fall. So we should turn our faces to the light and ignore the darkness, spend as little time as possible in life thinking about death, until it is thrust upon us and simply has to be faced.

However, there is a penalty that goes with that approach, fear of the unknown. Indeed it is perhaps more widely feared by this generation than it has ever been, largely perhaps because the consolations offered by religion are no longer anything like so widely accepted, or so effective. The process of dilution and erosion of religious influence has been going on over a long period, with the rising power and influence of science and technology in every aspect of our lives. We have by and large, moved away from the injunctions and the promises of religion, towards the proofs and the certainties of science. The loss has been that whereas religion talks to us a great deal about the meaning and the implications of death as part of life, science has virtually nothing to say about it. That is perhaps the greatest reason why today, death is almost universally feared and regarded as a tragedy, a great loss, rather than as the natural and human event that it is.

That is a view of death that is captured so accurately and so poignantly in Philip Larkin's celebrated poem, The Aubade.

"I work all day and get drunk all night.
Wake at four, to soundless dark I stare.
In time the curtain edges will grow light.
Till then see what's already there; Unresting death, a whole day nearer now.
Making all thought impossible but how, And where and when I shall myself die.
Arid interrogation: yet the dread of dying and of being dead Flashes afresh to hold and horrify.
The mind blanks at the glare. Not in remorse; The good not done, the love not given, time Torn off unused. Nor wretchedly because An only life can take so long to climb Clear of the wrong beginning, and may never.
But at the total emptiness forever, The sure extinction that we travel to And shall be lost in always. Not to be here Not to be anywhere
And soon; nothing more terrible. Nothing more true."

A truly fearful vision of emptiness at the end of life. But there is another factor that has, I think, become increasingly important, forcing people of all generations, young as well as old, to face up to the difficult questions posed by death. The fact is that medical science has become so powerful in terms of stretching out the last period of our life, when many of our faculties and physical abilities have become disabled, that we are confronted with a much longer period of time, often several years in fact, to contemplate the darkness of death. This is true both for older people who are dying, and for the younger people who have to watch their parents perhaps, going through the process of losing the faculties that make them knowable and recognizable as loved ones. For everybody concerned, it can be an immensely painful period that can leave deep scars on those who stay behind. For this reason, if for no other, it is good for us to look, without flinching, at the fact of death.

There are two main options that we have to consider. One might be called the Religious View, built up over many centuries of contemplation and revelation. The other is the Scientific View that has emerged in the last couple of hundred years or so, as science has steadily supplanted religion as a dominant force in society.

The Religious View: The Yearning for Immortality

All religions are essentially concerned to pass on their accumulated wisdom about the bits of our existence that we can't see and touch. Where we came from, the nature of our spiritual life while we are here, and where we journey to when we are gone. That is the very stuff of all religions. That is what they are about. Clearly no religion has a monopoly of the truth in these areas since they are, by definition, dealing with speculation. There can be nothing that resembles empirical proof. This is a key point that is often overlooked. We can quite rightly demand proof from scientific research since it is dealing by and large with what can be measured or weighed or observed. Thus we can fairly demand of scientific experiment, "Is it true or is it false?" As far as religions are concerned however, dealing with the unseen and the immeasurable as they do, that question is very wide of the mark. It makes far better sense to apply an altogether different yardstick, which might be best expressed as, "Does it work?"

That takes us back to one of the fundamental questions that has run like a thread throughout this book, about the *purpose* of religion in our lives. Does it work? That is to say, does it help us to live more complete lives? Does it help us to make judgements and take actions that increase the sum total of human happiness? Does it help us to die peacefully?

So we are talking essentially about speculation here, and there are two key points that seem to stand out. One is that we all have to face up to our mortality at some time or another, and even if the religious discussion about death lies at the margins of our lives it remains the cultural environment in which we grow up. At the very least, it encourages us to think about and thus come to terms with death in various ways. That background cultural environment undoubtedly has profound effects on the way we live our lives.

The second point is that virtually all religions teach that death is not an end point, a transition from life to absolute nothingness. All the major world religions offer the consolation of some form of continued spiritual life after death. The precise nature of that after life or continued life is fundamentally different, as you might expect, from religion to religion, but they all provide this huge, overwhelming promise of continuity, which has been such a strong theme throughout the entire history of human civilisation. It has become known as the yearning for immortality.

As we dig further and further into the past we see civilisation after civilisation that has buried its dead not simply with great reverence, but with the goods and chattels that they are going to need in the next life to re-establish their status, and to enable them to live in some comfort.

Today, the chattels have gone, but the core belief in immortality remains. Christian and Islamic tradition for example teaches a *single* life span for each unique individual, created and given by God, and a soul or spiritual essence that lives on after death for all eternity. Precisely what happens to the spiritual essence is very much dependant on the life that has been lived. It can either be in a place of punishment, Hell, or of reward, Heaven, or some intermediate place, Purgatory. Although it does seem that the modern Catholic Church is in the process of getting rid of purgatory as an idea.

Several Eastern or Asian religions such as Hinduism and including Buddhism, teach the dissolution of the physical identity but the eternal existence of a spiritual life force or "life entity" which reappears in life time after life time, and which is never extinguished.

There are very considerable doctrinal differences between the concept of the soul, and the life entity, but either way, some essential core of being is seen to achieve immortality.

The Scientific View of Death: The End

As we have seen, science doesn't have very much to say about death. It can talk very precisely about the conception and evolution of the foetus in the womb, and about the dissolution of the physical attributes of the body after death, but, understandably enough, it has nothing to say about anything that might be described as a soul, or the continued existence of a spiritual entity. They lie well beyond the scientific remit. But of course the implications of the scientific position don't end there. The scientific logic argues that when the body decays so too of course does the brain, and with it all the features that we normally associate with the brain, including for example the mind, and consciousness and memory and sense of self. All the elements, in short, that we are accustomed to use, in defining our unique individuality. Philosophers may talk of the mind in terms of our total capacity to think and feel, and most of us would be inclined to agree with that sort of idea. Our mind is wonderful, unique, everything that we are, everything that we think and feel and experience and desire. But scientists commonly describe the mind in terms of the movement of potassium and sodium ions across cell membranes. That may well be the case. I am not in a position to judge. But is anybody? All that we can say for sure is that cell membranes do not survive the body's dissolution.

So on that basis, the idea that some essential or spiritual self "escapes" from the body at the moment of death, and has a continued existence in some other environment is seen to be irrational and unscientific, and therefore very difficult to sustain. This is one of the main reasons for the argument that the accelerating march of science over the past 100 years, for all its unquestioned benefits, has played a key role in eroding the bed rock of a coherent spiritual philosophy in Western society. That in turn may lie at the heart of the uncertainty and instability and spiritual aimlessness that is so characteristic of contemporary society.

That having been said, it is a major irony, that many scientists who live their entire lives in the zealous pursuit of the rational and the definable, nevertheless still retain an unshakeable belief in the existence of some form of after life. An irony indeed, but also of course a source of great comfort to the rest of us. Man clearly cannot live by science alone!

Nevertheless, the rational scientific view does leave religious organisations open to the charge that their teachings about an after life are based not so much on insight, as on quite different motives, motives such as providing consolation and hope to ordinary people who fear the black emptiness of death along with Philip Larkin. Or alternatively, establishing a powerful moral lever for getting people to live better and more responsible lives in the here and now, so as to avoid divine punishment in the next.

The great revolution that split the Catholic Church asunder in the 16th century came about in part at least because the Church claimed to have special knowledge about death, and it was using it to manipulate people in life. It was selling vast numbers of bits of paper, called Papal Indulgences, on the promise that they would enable people to escape in the next life, the effects of their sins in this life. From this universal manipulation was born the schism of the Reformation.

This raises the key issue that really lies at the heart of this whole debate, and which is profoundly important to all of us, namely, the effect that our attitude to death has on the way we live out our lives here on earth. We may think it has no effect. It does, profoundly.

A Matter of Life and Death

In Medieval times, when the influence of the Catholic Church was at its height in Europe, every church would have displayed in a prominent place right inside the front porch, so-called Doom paintings. These were pictures that displayed in graphic detail the blissful rewards in Heaven, or the fierce punishments to be meted out in Hell, for good deeds or bad ones, committed in this life. These pictures weren't in any way marginal, they weren't simply decorative. They were a crucially important method for the Church to get its central message across to ordinary people who couldn't read. The Church wanted the view of *death* they represented to affect profoundly, the way people *lived.*

Times have changed radically, but has human nature? It is being demanded of doctor scientists these days, that they be more exact than they have ever been, in defining the precise moment when the spark of life is struck in the foetus, and when it is extinguished in the dying. America was split right down the middle, from the man in the street all the way up to the President himself, when, in 2005, the feeding tube was removed from the throat of the young paralysed woman, Terri Schiavo. Why? Because it brought the stark choice into everyone's home, between what we know, life and light, even a life so sadly diminished, and death and the great unknown.

One might argue for example that the modern horror of the suicide bomber who is prepared to destroy his or her life for a cause, can *only exist* because there is the notion around, rightly or wrongly, that a death in such circumstances provides an instant passage to some paradise in which they will live on in perfect bliss. Let me hasten to underline those words, *"rightly or wrongly."* I have read and studied the Quran with Islamic teachers, during a period when I was living and working in the Middle East, but I am in no position to say whether or not that promise exists in its pages, and I wouldn't in any way wish to suggest that. As far as one can judge the various Islamic authorities also seem to be split on the issue. But there is no doubt that whatever the truth of the matter, the notion is around in some form, even if only in the form of propaganda, and it clearly serves in some measure, to fuel the recruitment of young people prepared to give up their lives in this extraordinary way. In that sense, there can be no doubt, I think, that their view of *death* profoundly influences the way they *live.*

To take a more everyday and less extreme example, if one's view of death is that it is the ultimate end, that there is nothing that comes after, then it is not difficult to imagine that it could well induce a self-centred, short-term, make-hay-while-the-sun-shines approach to life. A life focused largely on material acquisition and display, with very little if any concern, for the impact on others or on the world about us. Keeping up with the Jones' family, or doing rather better than them, could well become the key focus of one's existence. Many would argue that this is, in many ways, *the distinguishing hallmark* of today's society, a rampant, even desperate consumerism that is even prepared to countenance the destruction of the environment that keeps us all alive.

Since death, in this scenario, would mean the ultimate loss and denial of everything that one had lived for in terms of material possession, the approach to death would be a fearful and a stressful time. It could be seen *only* from the standpoint of loss. Indeed there is the well worn phrase, coined specifically to describe just how we should live in response to this desperate situation, *"You can't take it with you,"* it reminds us. The clear implication being that we need to spend, and rush about having a good time in a sort of manic bid to cram everything in before the ultimate end. Lest we should be tempted to believe that this is essentially a modern situation, brought into being by the conspicuous consumption of the past century or so, Nichiren Daishonin writes compassionately and beautifully to people around him facing the same, very human dilemma,

"Though you may move among the most exalted company of court nobles, your hair done up elegantly like clouds and your sleeves fluttering like eddies of snow, such pleasures, when you stop to consider them, are no more than a dream within a dream. You must come to rest at last under the carpet of weeds at the foot of the hill, and all your jewelled daisies and brocade hangings will mean nothing to you on the road to the afterlife."*

Conversely, if the approach to death is that it is, above all, a time of *judgement,* when the struggles to cope with the pleasures and pains and temptations of earthly life will be held in the balance so to speak, by the supreme god who created all life, then one might argue the effect of that in several ways. It could be seen as providing a lifeline so strong and so clear in its definition, that it could carry you through all of life's troubles with an unwavering vision of a wonderful afterlife. Or it could perhaps become a source of fear and foreboding and guilt that could cast a powerful shadow over the later years of your life. When Pope John Paul died in April of 2005, the edition of *Time* Magazine that covered the event, carried a striking caption on one of the key pictures. It read, *"The Pope made sure his message was clear: that life is God's alone to give...and to take".* It would be difficult would it not, to cling to such a view of death, without it having a powerful ripple effect throughout one's life?

It is for Us to Choose

So where does this admittedly brief discussion of the two main options, the religious and the scientific view of life after death, leave us? There are three main points I would want to make.

One is that, however dominant a force science is in modern society, it would be unwise to let it have the last word on the nature of death, since death lies beyond its remit. Science simply does not claim to be in a position, to pronounce on matters of spirituality, or the nature of eternity, among many others. It chooses to express its authority only in those areas that have yielded to scientific investigation. Daisaku Ikeda has put it very succinctly.

"Scientific theories are subject to, and must be subjected to, theoretical and experimental tests of validity. Ways of evaluating religious hypotheses however are different. First religious hypotheses must be judged on how well they explain the phenomenon of life to unaided human intelligence. Second they must be judged on how effective they are in providing a foundation for human judgement and action. In other words, we must ask whether scientific hypotheses are true, whereas we must ask whether religious hypotheses have any value for the improvement of the qualities of humanity." *

The second point is that the idea of an after life, of one kind or another, can claim powerful longevity. In one form or another it has persisted throughout all of human history. It has taken similar forms in vastly different cultures and widely separated societies. That persistence does not of course deliver a proof or a validation. By definition that is unknowable. We are dealing with speculation. All the persistence proves is that these ideas meet some deeply felt need in the human psyche. They are, one might argue, an essential part of our humanity.

And the third point is that these ideas may be speculation, but they are also profoundly beneficial, even, it could be argued, on an evolutionary scale. Man is essentially a social animal. He has only been able to survive and flourish in social groups. The idea that there is an after life, and that it is profoundly affected by the way we live our current lives, has immense social implications. Not only can it provide a core of inner strength and resilience for the individual during difficult and challenging times, but it clearly encourages *social* qualities that are extremely difficult to explain in evolutionary terms, such as altruism and caring for others, and acts of unselfishness.

From this standpoint the religious concept of an eternal life has extraordinary power to improve the quality of human life. It holds out the constant promise that actions that create value for *others* as well as oneself, actions that support and uphold *others* within the group, will undoubtedly bring benefits in the "life" to come. Meanwhile of course, they undoubtedly boost the survivability and the quality of life of the group as a whole.

It thus meets precisely the criterion that Daisaku Ikeda outlined in the quotation above, namely,

"… we must ask whether scientific hypotheses are true, whereas we must ask whether religious hypotheses have any value for the improvement of the qualities of humanity."

It is in that context that we can examine the Buddhist view of life and death.

CHAPTER FOURTEEN

The Buddhist View of Eternal Life

It has often been said that the profound problems posed by death lie at the heart of Buddhist philosophy. That is clearly borne out in the life stories of both Shakyamuni Buddha and Nichiren Daishonin. Shakyamuni left his home and family because he was so moved by the great sufferings he saw attaching to life around him, in particular to old age, sickness and death. He felt he had to resolve these issues in some way, so that he could then help ordinary people to overcome the problems that they posed. Similarly, when Nichiren entered a monastery at a very young age of 12 or so, he was so moved by the suffering caused to ordinary people by the sheer confusion of teachings around, and he too focused on the mystery posed by death. He felt that he could not properly approach the sufferings of life until he understood the mystery of death.

The implication for us would seem to be clear, namely that although it isn't necessary to believe in the idea of reincarnation to begin to practice Buddhism, it is important to get to grips in some way, with the Buddhist view of death and its relationship to life.

Buddhism teaches the eternity of life, that all forms of life, including human beings, are born, and that those forms of life die, but that the life force within them goes on forever. That is to say there is no creation of matter, and no annihilation. What is quite extraordinary about that teaching is its modernity, in the sense that fundamental to modern physics also, is the concept that there can be no creation and no destruction of energy. There is a set of physical laws that goes by the somewhat unwieldy title of the Laws of Conservation of Energy and Matter. They propose, very briefly, that all the matter and all the energy in the universe is a fixed quantity. It can't be increased, nor can it be reduced. It is however constantly *interchangeable,* so that it can change from one *form* to another or from one state to another, in a constant eternal cycle.

So, to give an everyday example, the heat energy of the Sun can combine with various nutrients from the soil to produce, from a tiny seedling, at first a sapling and eventually, over the succeeding decades, a huge forest tree. That tree might be cut down in its prime and cut up into logs and burned, producing a certain amount of heat and light in the process, and a pile of ash. The *form* of the matter and the energy has thus changed radically, but at the end of the process, science tells us, the *sum total* of all the matter and the heat and the light energy involved in these processes remains constant. Nothing is lost and nothing is gained.

Alternatively that same tree might grow and flourish for many, many years before being toppled by some tempest and slowly beginning to decompose back into the forest floor. During that period of decay it would certainly become the home and the source of food for whole colonies of other living things from microbes and insects, to mosses and lichens, each one of which would go through that same cycle of birth and maturation, decline and death. All that would be different in each case would be the time scale, a matter of months perhaps for some of the insects, a few years for the mosses and lichens, a few hundred years for the tree itself. But the essential point is that at each stage of the process, the matter and energy has simply changed its form from one state to another. When all the sums are done, when all the transformations of energy and matter are taken into account, science tells us once again, that *nothing* has been added to the total of energy and matter already existing in the universe and *nothing* has been lost or escaped from the universe. Many life forms have been born, and many life forms have died, but the sum total of energy and matter in the universe remains the same.

The extraordinary thing, as I have said, is that Buddhism teaches almost exactly the same concept. Although, of course it is important to emphasize that Buddhism does not in any way seek the validation of science, any more than science seeks to buttress the teachings of religion. It is unquestionably remarkable, that through the inexplicable nature of his enlightenment, Shakyamuni was teaching the law of conservation of energy and matter many hundreds of years before it had a name.

Continuity and Renewal

So squeezed into a nutshell, the Buddhist principle of the eternity of life embodies this central idea of continuity and renewal.

Death is seen in Buddhism to be not an end, but a period of rest. Or to put it another way, what we call life is not *one*, but *two* states. It has periods of active, manifest existence on this earth, and periods of rest or latency, that we call death. Buddhism describes these periods of latency as neither existence nor non-existence, where the life force or the life energy that was inherent in our life, sinks back so to speak into the ocean of life energy that fills the universe. Our life energy, or 'life entity' alternates between these two states in a constantly repeated cycle. Thus, central to Buddhism is the idea that in every period of life, there is the potential of death, and in every period of death there is the potential of the next life. Nothing is created, nothing is destroyed. In each period of active, manifest life, our lives follow the fundamental cycle that is common to everything in the universe, indeed to the very universe itself, we are born, we grow, we decline and we die. The life energy in our life then simply changes its state, flowing smoothly from death, into the state of latency, ready to flow smoothly again into a new life.

Nichiren repeatedly sought to describe this sense of *continuity* in his letters to his followers, talking of life and death, as we know it, being the two functions of eternal life.

The analogy that comes closest to hand, and with which we are instantly familiar is the constantly repeated cycle of waking and sleeping. We get up in the morning and launch ourselves into all kinds of activity with renewed energy. We travel about, we relate to other people, respond to problems and challenges, ponder over some things and take decisions about others. We laugh and cry perhaps, experience anger and jubilation, and then, late in the evening, when we've had enough for the time being of both thinking and doing, we call it a day and go to sleep.

During genuine, deep sleep we essentially vacate our lives. We are, to all intents and purposes, unconscious. We may dream of course, but we don't *initiate* thoughts or actions. Although we all take the business of sleep very much for granted, to scientists it is still very much a mystery. It is such a different state of being. So different indeed that it is still pretty much an enigma to scientists as to what its key function is and just how it relates to the "waking" us. They still cannot identify, for example, any vital *biological* function that is restored by sleep. The muscles of the body for example don't seem to need sleep, just intermittent periods of relaxation. The closest researchers have come to identifying a purpose is that it seems to serve in some way to refresh the brain, and give it time to consolidate all the streams of information it has gathered while awake.

That having been said, one of the few things that *is* clear in the general mystery, is that sleep is absolutely universal and vital. Throughout the animal kingdom from top to bottom, from the mighty blue whale, even down to the humble fruit fly, everything has to have its periods of sleep. So that sleep ranks with food and water, as an essential ingredient for life. Moreover, if human beings put off sleep for any extended period they become progressively unable to function as a coherent, active animal, until the brain simply crashes, like an overburdened computer, and refuses to go on. We *have* to sleep.

And having slept, we rise again and launch ourselves into all kinds of activity with renewed energy. We travel about, we relate to other people etc… etc…. Thus sleep is not simply the *absence* of thought and action, it may be regarded as a different state of being, and in that sense our ordinary daily lives have *two* clearly defined and markedly different phases, one of activity, and one of rest. They are so to speak, two aspects of the same human being. In a similar way,

Buddhism teaches, both life and death are the two phases of life, inherent in ordinary human life.

Seen from this perspective, death is not a wholly different phenomenon. Still less is it an end or an annihilation. It is a different state of being. Buddhism uses the phrase "neither existence nor non existence," to describe it. There is no precise parallel in English so we tend to use this word "latency."

Just as the state of sleep is so different from waking, that scientists can still only come up with hypotheses, or guesses, about its true nature and purpose, so, in very much the same way, we shouldn't in any way feel uncomfortable about the fact that we find it difficult to get our minds round this concept of *"neither existence nor non existence"*. It is a field in which there is, by definition, much speculation, but little certainty. The most important point perhaps is that we should grapple with the issue so that we both deepen our understanding, and lessen our fear.

All that has been said so far may be all very well for the believer, and very comforting for the fearful human spirit. But, one can hear the confirmed sceptic demand, "What precisely is the nature of the bit that is everlasting?"

That is the crucial question, is it not? The fact is that the only part of the process of which we have *certain* knowledge is that the particular parcel of proteins and chemicals, that makes up the physical body that is called John Brown, is destined to disintegrate and decompose shortly after death. That is beyond doubt, and we know that that process includes all the functioning elements so essential to the sense of self, such as brain and memory. So in what sense can some essential part of John Brown be described as being involved in an everlasting process?

The Nature of Identity

The Christian view of life and death is very familiar to us, but it is worth restating it briefly in order to highlight the differences between it and the Buddhist view. Essentially Christianity teaches that very close to the time when sperm and egg come together God creates a unique life, into which he implants a unique spiritual essence called a soul. When the individual life comes to an end in death, the soul that is *unique* to it and wholly identified with it, lives on eternally in either Heaven or Hell or the in-between place called Purgatory. According to this view, which lies at the very basis of Western culture, each individual has only *one* physical life here on earth, and that the events that take place during that one life govern what happens to the soul for all of eternity.

By contrast Buddhism does not have the concept of the soul, nor does it accept that there is a process that we might call creation, since all matter and all energy already exist in the universe and nothing can be added. Instead there is the essential concept of a parcel of life energy, or a *life entity.* During the phase of life, an individual life entity, unites with the necessary essential elements or components, to form an individual. At death those elements or components separate or disassociate, and the life entity moves off and begins a period of latency. When the conditions are right, it unites and appears once more with another set of essential elements to form *another* individual life. And on and on, throughout all eternity.

Buddhism describes the essential elements that come together when the sperm fertilises the egg or when the individual life begins, as The Five Components. It is important to remember that the Five Components define the *whole* being, both the physical and the spiritual aspects of the individual's life, since as we have seen, in Buddhism, the physical and the spiritual are inseparable. So, very briefly The Five Components are defined as follows;

- *Form*, or the physical body, and the sensors or senses that we have to enable us to receive a continuous stream of information about our environment.
- *Perception*, or the process of receiving that flow of information through our senses and putting it together to make sense of what is going on around us.
- *Conception* is the in-built ability we have to do that, to go on interpreting all the information we are receiving all the time, and to unscramble it so that it makes sense to us.
- *Volition*, is the ability to initiate action on the basis of our continuing stream of interpretations.
- *Consciousness* is in a sense the over-arching ability to go on doing all those things, receive information, comprehend its physical and its emotional dimensions, make judgements and decisions about it, and initiate actions in response to it.

The Five Components come together to define each individual life, and they stay together in a constant process of change and interaction as the individual moves through his or her period of active life. As we all know to our chagrin, our "form," or our appearance changes radically as we go through life, to the extent that we may become scarcely recognisable as the youth we once were. We change in every conceivable way as we grow older, even most of our cells change completely every seven years or so, and yet, we know that at the heart of our lives there resides our essential self, recognizable, and knowable to all our friends.

There are many points that could be made about this concept of the Five Components, but two seem to me to be essential to a basic understanding. One is that the coming together of the Five Components is a purely *temporary* matter. They only stay together for as long as our life lasts. It is known indeed as the Truth of Temporary Existence, which expresses not simply the fleeting brevity of human life, but the essential fact that each life entity represents a *unique* fusion of the Five Components. They do not come together *in that way* ever again, because the causes and the conditions that were the basis for that life can never be the same. Thus having come together to form the life entity of John Brown, after John Brown's demise, the Five Components will not come together to form John Brown again.

Death in Buddhism is defined as the moment when the interaction between the Five Components that began in the womb comes to an end. It may be that death comes in a single, clearly defined moment, such as a car accident or, through a long period of decline as the ageing body slowly loses its ability to function. In either case, as soon as the *Form*, or the body, is no longer able to hold together the other components, conception, perception, volition, and consciousness, they disassociate. That unique life is at an end. The parcel of life force that was inherent in it, slips away and enters into a period of latency.

The second point, and this may come as something of a surprise, is that there is nothing in this Buddhist description of life that is essentially at odds with scientific explanations of life. We have already looked briefly at the fact that the laws of physics describe a universe which is remarkably in keeping with the fundamental Buddhist view, in which energy and matter cannot be either created or destroyed, they can only change their state. But in addition to that, modern science of course also describes life as the *temporary* coming together of a relatively limited number of essential elements and compounds. Taken in isolation, as separate atoms and molecules, they cannot be said to have anything that might be called "life." But once they have come together, they grow and differentiate in ways that are still only partially understood, to form a living individual, who is endowed with the most complex physical and emotional and intellectual potential, for a relatively brief period of time, three score years and ten or thereabouts. When the endowment has run its brief course, the atoms and molecules that had united so closely to form a particular and individual life, revert to their original status and disassociate, as inanimate raw materials. They don't disappear, they simply disassociate, ready to be put together into some other form. They are, that is, recycled.

That doesn't sound so radically different, does it, from the idea of the Five Components?

The Dilemma of Memory
But that brings us to a closer look at how Buddhism defines consciousness, since that clearly has a crucial part to play in our understanding of what it is that lives on eternally. Buddhism defines no less than nine levels of consciousness. At first glance nine levels may sound very different from the broad descriptions that we are accustomed to in modern western studies of the mind at work, but in fact, even a brief analysis reveals that there are very considerable overlaps and similarities. Very briefly, the nine Buddhist levels are made up as follows;

- The first Five levels are equivalent to the five senses of sight, smell, hearing, taste and touch. These are the sensory levels that enable us to acquire a constant stream of information about our surroundings.

- The Sixth level essentially represents the immediate, instinctive integration and management of that information, so that we can co-ordinate the separate inputs from our sense, the sights and sounds and smells and so on, and construct from them a marvellously detailed and constantly moving assembly of pictures of what's going on close to and further away.

- The Seventh level, which is sometimes known as the *mano* or *discerning* level, isn't directly related to sensory input however, it draws upon our inner world. It is, so to speak, the thinking part of our mind. This the part of our mind that might be equated with the famous expression from the seventeenth century French philosopher, Descartes, *'I think therefore I am.'* So it has some measure of equivalence to the Freudian concept of ego, although it was formulated around 2500 years before Freud was at work. It is involved with such things as self-awareness and self esteem, and taste and judgement and sense of right or wrong, based upon our inner store of knowledge and experience, as well as our reading of the current information being organised by the sixth consciousness.

When we are up and around during the day we are operating essentially on the basis of these seven levels of consciousness. They enable us to drive a car accurately, or cross the road *after* the bus has passed, make our way to the work place or to the supermarket and so on. All the time of course we are receiving this vast torrent of sensory input through our five senses, a continuous bombardment of information at every level. The sixth level ensures that we sort it all out, almost without giving it a moment's thought, to enable us to make the right movements and responses, at the right time. And while we are navigating our way through the day in this way, the seventh level has the freedom and the capacity, to be contemplating something completely unrelated to what we might happen to be doing, from profound philosophical thoughts to the shopping list for tonight's dinner party.

- The Eighth level goes deeper still, it lies below the level of our waking mind, so that when we are active during the day it lies buried you might say, beneath the activities of the first seven levels. It's only when we are deeply asleep, and the conscious mind is therefore dormant, that the Eighth level emerges into 'activity.' Buddhism in fact teaches that our dreams are likely to be made up from the random thoughts and actions 'released' from the Eighth level.

It is known as the *alaya* consciousness and it is often described as the storehouse of our minds, a vast endless repository of all that we have encountered and experienced with our first seven levels of consciousness, whether we are actually 'conscious' of having experienced them, or not. A key point is that nothing that has occurred in our thoughts or words or deeds escapes the Eighth consciousness. That is crucially important since, as we have seen above, we make *causes* at all three levels, thoughts words and deeds. Thus above all, Buddhism teaches, this Eighth region stores all the causes that we have made and all the effects that we have gathered, not only through this life, but mystically, through all previous lives as well. In this sense, then, the alaya consciousness opens a window onto precisely what it is, and, no less important, what it is not, that continues through death and latency into another life.

Before I continue with this central issue that we are pursuing, let me briefly round off the description of the nine levels of consciousness.

- The Ninth level or the *amala* consciousness is held to be the pure and fundamental life force at the very core of our lives, free from karmic effects. It is equated with the inexhaustible life force of the universe, which sustains us in our lives, and of which our lives are seen to be a manifestation. Thus the Ninth consciousness is held in Nichiren Buddhism, to be the fundamental source of the energy for all our physical and intellectual and spiritual activity, and a resource that we seek to tap into with the chanting that lies at the heart of the practice. One of the main functions of chanting is indeed to raise our life force.

But back to the Eighth consciousness, in the context of the Buddhist teaching on the eternity of life, how does the vast storehouse of all our experiences, all our causes and effects, held in the alaya consciousness, relate to what we know in our everyday lives as our memory?

Memory is clearly crucially important to our sense of self. It represents the accumulation of experience and knowledge that defines us. It describes to us the route we have followed and explains why we are at this point in our life journey. Studies of people who have lost their memory or, worse still, those rare cases of people who are unable to form memories of their actions from day to day, describe individuals who are in a sense, lost in space and time, with no sense of past, deprived of a core sense of self.

Put simply, it is memory that ensures that no matter how radical the physical and mental changes that take place in our lives, as we make the transition from nine to ninety, we continue to *know* that we are the same person.

At this ordinary everyday level Buddhism does not teach that the life entity that re-emerges from a period of latency into a new life, carries with it any *memory* of a previous life. The life entity that informed the life of the individual known as John Brown for example, carried no memory of any *previous life*. In the same way, after John Brown's demise, when that life entity re-emerges from latency into a new phase of existence at some later date, it will not carry any memory of John Brown's life. It will carry however Buddhism tells us, all the *causes* and all the *effects* of John Brown's existence, stored up in the alaya consciousness.

The distinction is of course crucial. It means that we must try to understand the distinction between *life entity* on the one hand, which Buddhism teaches is eternal, and *individual identity* on the other, which Buddhism teaches is short lived, the truth of temporary existence indeed.

Understanding Identity

Put at its simplest, this means that William's unique and essential identity, my appearance and my character, are temporary. The person whom I know myself to be, no matter what changes take place in my appearance and personality as I journey through three score years and ten, is attached to *this* unique individual. It is built up of the memories and the experiences, the causes and the effects, that I have accumulated through *this* life. It is as temporary as this life itself is. It dies with William at the point of death.

The *life entity* on the other hand, or the parcel of universal life energy that now informs William's life, sometimes called the *innate* self, lying below self knowledge, will, when William's unique identity comes to an end, pass into a period of "neither existence nor non existence." Then, at some time in the future, when the conditions are right, it will become manifest again in another unique individual identity. That individual identity will also develop his or her own unique and essential sense of self, which again will be purely temporary, and die when that individual identity comes to the end of his or her life. It will *not* be William 2.

In this sense then, the life entity, the raw life force, goes on from lifetime to lifetime. It is neither created nor destroyed. It exists before each birth, and continues to exist after each death. In each period of existence, Buddhism teaches, it gathers a new accumulation of causes and effects.

That accumulated cargo of causes and effects carried within the eighth consciousness, lies below the level of the waking mind, so that each successive life form involved, each individual if you wish, will have no conscious awareness and no memory of it. Nonetheless, Buddhism teaches that those accumulated causes and effects lying in the alaya consciousness, will have a *profound* effect on the actions, the thoughts and word and deeds of the life entity in the next period of existence. This is the basis, in Buddhist teachings for so many of the differences in circumstances between individuals, and for many of the inexplicable effects that occur during our lives. They are effects related to distant causes attaching to the life entity.

However, within the span of each lifetime the change of *identity* is complete and total. Each one is totally different from the previous one, and crucially, each one has no *memory* of what went before.

Needless to say, this distinction is not at all easy to grasp. Inevitably, since we are dealing with the unknowable and the unseeable, it remains slippery and elusive however painstakingly one tries to sift through the arguments. And the fact is of course, that in the daily reality of our lives we don't often have to grapple with it.

A metaphor that one might hang on to is that of waves formed on the great face of the ocean. Picture a vast army of waves lifting and surging across the face of the ocean as far as the eye can see and beyond. Each wave may resemble its neighbour, but close to, each one is going to be subtly different and unique, with its own individual features and contours. Although it may seem to be just one of a vast army, each wave has been formed around its own *unique* parcel of energy that has lifted it up and brought it into existence. The wave travels for a time, and then slowly collapses and sinks back into the ocean from which it came. The unique *identity* of the wave has gone. That particular wave, with those unique characteristics, will *never* form again. The parcel of energy that formed it however, has sunk back into the vast body of energy that surges within the ocean. It will remain there, unchanged, in a state that we might call latency. And then, when the conditions are right, it will combine again with the components of the sea water to lift another wave, which will have its own minutely unique shape and form and characteristics. And on and on, through all eternity. The parcel of energy, the life entity, the innate self, remains the same from existence to existence. Each successive wave, or form that it energises, is a different and wholly temporary *identity*.

The image of the wave may help to fix the idea in the mind, but it does not of course *explain* anything. Nor can it. We are, as we have already said, dealing here with what is essentially unknowable. But that having been said, it does make sense. It has a logical consistency. Buddhism is reason, and there is nothing in this explanation that is at odds with what is known and understood about the cycles of existence that shape the universe. That is a crucial point.

Buddhism does not ask us to come to terms with the reality of death in order to cast a fearful shadow over our lives. Indeed the reverse is true. By grappling with the Buddhist ideas on the eternity of life, it becomes possible to see death not as a thing apart, a vast and fearful emptiness, but as a continuity, as a natural part of the cycle that underpins all things. As natural, and as welcome indeed as the period of sleep that refreshes and reenergizes us, between each period of waking.

Buddhism places our individual human lives right at the centre of the unending universal cycle that encompasses everything, the cycle of birth and growth and decline and death. We acknowledge that all physical existence is temporary. We accept that all energy in the universe, including the life energy that informs living things is eternal. Buddhism places our cycles of birth and death firmly within that context.

CHAPTER FIFTEEN

Approaching The Practice

It is important to de-mystify this word practice. The fact is that it is used in very much the same way as one might use it in talking about any other field of human endeavour. The basic objective of any practice is to get *better* at something. Any sportsman, any musician, any artist knows that unless they train, unless they practice, they cannot possibly attain their full potential. Moreover, having more *innate* talent doesn't mean less training. The bigger the talent, the more, rather than the less, those sportsmen and musicians have to train because they have a greater potential to fulfil. Few people train as hard as top class olympic athletes or concert pianists for example.

By the same token, however inherent the quality of Buddhahood may be, drawing it out into the light of our daily lives requires a real personal commitment to sustained practice.

As the famous, world-class golfer Gary Player once said, *"The more I practice the luckier I get!"*

In my experience something very similar is true of Buddhism. You will frequently hear Buddhists say that the more they practice the more they feel themselves to be fortunate, in harmony with themselves and in some way, however difficult it may be to define, in rhythm with the world around them. Unexpected opportunities appear, for example, at the most opportune moment, seemingly insoluble problems suddenly unravel, relationships improve, anxieties diminish. That may sound just too good to be true. That doesn't alter the fact however that they continue to occur. Similarly when Buddhists are aware that they are approaching a time of extra stress or difficulties in their lives, a set of important exams coming up, or stress in a close relationship, or illness or a change of job, they go into training you might say. They deliberately step up their practice, to give themselves the greater resilience and wisdom and self confidence, to be able to see their way through a difficult time, and to help them to drive through the greater turbulence in their environment.

It is as deliberate and conscious a process as that.

Thus people use the practice as an additional asset available to them. Buddhism *is* daily life. In many ways that simple-sounding phrase is the very heart of the Buddhist message. Trying to learn how to see the problems and the challenges that come ceaselessly, from all directions, as *opportunities*, opportunities to grow our lives. If you think about it for a moment, that necessarily means developing the wisdom to spot them, and the courage to grab onto them, because exploiting opportunities inevitably means change, and change takes courage.

In a sense it is rather like the Chinese pictograms that represent the concept of crisis. In fact precisely the same pictograms have two meanings, one meaning is *crisis,* the other is *opportunity.* It thus becomes a question of perception. If we perceive the situation as a crisis it threatens to knock us down and steal our hope. If we see it as an opportunity it lifts us up and spurs us on. The situation itself is no different. The only difference lies in our perception, our attitude to the situation. But that difference makes all the difference, since it empowers us to achieve a radically different *outcome.*

The Buddhist argument essentially is that they are not going to stop coming, those problems. It's a bit like saying something as patently obvious as, water is wet. That's just the way things are. The only part of the equation over which we have control is our *approach* to those problems, and the key stage in the process of change is coming to understand that this is not a purely intellectual process. Buddhism suggests that the intellect can only take us so far. We can't simply *think* our way into a radical new approach to life, we have to work at it, we have to train, to acquire that difference of perspective.

That is not an easy truth, either to believe in or to understand. It is not something we are accustomed to doing. If we get a problem the immediate, instinctive, conditioned response is to go to brain. That's what we have always done. That, we believe, is where the powerhouse is. We are accustomed in the West, trained even, to live our lives driven by three primary engines; our intellect and our emotions, how we think and how we feel, and by our persona, or how we look and present ourselves. We place huge store, as indeed we should, on our intellectual ability to think our way through life problems. We attach immense value to emotional expression, and perhaps far too much to externals, to physical appearance.

Essentially all Buddhism is saying is, hang on a bit, there's more…there is a spiritual resource within you that is capable of lifting your life performance to a new level. Your Buddha nature.

Three Basic Elements

There are three basic elements to the practice of Nichiren Daishonin's Buddhism.

The basic practice is chanting, chanting the phrase Nam-myoho-renge-kyo out loud, rather than repeating a mantra silently within your head. The key point is that it is clearly a physical action and it has clear physiological effects. It involves moving considerable volumes of air into and out of the lungs for example, and it raises the body temperature. People regularly loosen their tie or take off their jacket when they are chanting. There are many who say that it's very good for the complexion for example because it powerfully stimulates the circulation and sets the skin tingling.

But above all it is a wonderful and joyful sound, and it is absolutely central to this practice. It is without question the essential driving force, the engine, without which the process of change simply cannot be achieved. Normally it is carried out twice a day. In the morning, to launch you into the day with a wholly positive, up beat frame of mind, and in the evening basically in the spirit of gratitude for the day that we've had, good, bad or indifferent. If it has been good there is a lot to be grateful for. If it has been bad then you may need to regain the courage and the confidence to tackle the challenges that have arisen. Both morning and evening it is accompanied by the recitation of two brief passages of the Lotus Sutra that are concerned with the universality of Buddhahood, and the eternity of life.

There is no set time to chant, nor any set period of chanting. As with so many other aspects of Buddhist practice, that is entirely up to the individual. It's your life. You can chant for as little time as you can spare before you have to catch the 8.10

train to the office, or "to your hearts content," as one of Nichiren's letters puts it. The practice is immensely flexible, shaped to fit in with the demands of a modern life. The key element is the *regularity* of the practice. Just as we need to refuel our bodies with meals two or three times a day, so we need this regular refreshment of our spiritual resources.

What do we think about when we chant? Well the short answer is not a lot. The intention if you like, is to become one with the rhythm of it, listen to the sound, feel the vibration. Enjoy the moment for it's own sake. Give the sound your full attention. The time for thought is before you start, what is it you want to chant about, and after you have finished, when the mind is clear, and you are deciding on what action you need to take. What do we chant for? We are chanting essentially to tap into this potential within our lives that will enable us to achieve a higher life condition. Daisaku Ikeda describes that potential as limitless, so that is the dominant underlying thought. But you can chant for any goal you wish to achieve either in the short or long term in your life, and the lives of those around you.

The fact is that people don't often start chanting because they want to 'save the planet,' so to speak, or rarely. They are more likely to start chanting for reasons that are much more personal, and closer to their daily life, sometimes outlandish, sometimes selfish. A better house for example, a better job, better health, a happy and successful day. Many people chant for these and other utterly normal worldly desires every day of the week. They are very much part of our ordinary humanity, and the desire for them is real enough. But the common experience is that the very process of chanting Nam-myoho–renge-kyo begins to broaden and deepen our view, and although these desires may stay, they begin to be changed and refined and added to. They grow dynamically just as our life grows, the initial desires serving as the seed, the primary cause, that drives people towards a greater self knowledge. It is in that sense that earthly desires may be said to lead to self enlightenment.

Chanting to achieve things in one's life, including material things, runs counter to a widely held perception of Buddhism, that it is essentially about *renunciation*, about giving up most worldly things as a necessary step on the road to achieving a higher spiritual condition. Nichiren Buddhism however teaches that renunciation, giving up things, *of itself*, brings no benefits. It argues that desire is basic to all human life and that as long as there is life there will be the instinctive desire in the hearts of all men and women to make the most of that life; to live, to grow, to love, to have.

Nichiren saw with great clarity that little was to be gained from people expending huge amounts of thought and time and energy seeking to extinguish a force that lay right at the core of their lives. On the contrary, infinitely more is to be achieved, by accepting it as an essential part of everyone's humanity, and *harnessing* it, as a powerful engine for individual development.

But let's be clear, we are not talking about a wholly rational process. It is in many ways beyond the reach of the intellect alone. There are many stories to be told of people who started chanting in this somewhat inconsequential way, driven purely by personal desires, more often than not, without any strong belief in the value of the practice. They now look back and often laugh openly at those somewhat shallow beginnings, in the knowledge of how profoundly their lives and their concerns have been changed. They continue to chant for their personal desires but now with a far wider horizon that extends from their personal on-going human revolution, outwards in ever increasing circles, to take in family and friends and workplace and community and the global society. The ultimate goal of the Nichiren Buddhist is a world made up of people and communities that live in peace one with another. We chant for it and work for it on a daily basis.

The second major element in the practice is study, studying a wide range of things from the letters and other writings of Nichiren Daishonin himself, to commentaries by Buddhist scholars, and accounts by individual Buddhists on the way in which the practice has affected their lives. There is I have to say a huge abundance of material, because it is such a broad ranging philosophy. That having been said, this is not an intellectual practice. The study is not about acquiring knowledge in an essentially egocentric way, as an end in itself, but about deepening one's understanding of the principles that inform the practice. Nichiren makes no bones about its importance. Indeed he goes so far as to say,

*"Exert yourself in the two ways of practice and study. Without practice and study there is no Buddhism."**

The third pillar of the practice is taking action, the struggle to fold Buddhist principles and values into the warp and weft of one's daily life, so that they are lived, rather than just perceived or understood. That is a daily struggle. Few things are more difficult to change than ingrained, unconscious patterns of thought and behaviour, driven by anger perhaps, or selfishness or basic lack of concern for other people's needs. That is part of all our experience. The Buddhist practice drives the inner transformation towards a fundamental respect for one's own life, and out of that grows respect for the lives of all others. But it is not of course a one-way journey, one step forward two steps back is a common experience.

But it is important to emphasise the point that we have touched upon previously, namely that Buddhism is not a morality. That is to say, it does not depend for its moral force on a prescribed set of behaviour or practices. It relies rather on the power of this inner transformation, on people learning how to accept responsibility for their own lives and their own actions. This clearly has the potential for far reaching effects not solely on the person at the centre, but on the whole of the society he or she inhabits.

The process begins with the individual. It all begins with the personal determination to change one's own life, but the effect of the changes we make in our thinking and therefore in our behaviour extend way beyond our own life. Indeed, since Buddhism draws no distinction between the individual, and the world around him, the environment in which he lives, the influence spreads out in an ever-widening, never-ending series of ripples.

Since the chanting of the phrase *Nam-myoho-renge Kyo* is central to this process, what does this phrase mean and where does it come from?

The Meaning Of Nam-Myoho-Renge-Kyo

Most of it comes from the Lotus Sutra itself. Myoho renge-kyo is the title of the Lotus Sutra in classical Japanese. It is written in the Chinese pictograms that the Japanese adopted as their own, in order to create their own written language.

The five characters used mean literally "The Mystic Law of the Lotus Sutra."

The word Nam, which is placed in front of the invocation is the committal word. It comes from the ancient language of Sanskrit and means, "to devote ones life to." So a straightforward literal translation of Nam-myoho-renge-kyo would be "I devote my life to the Mystic Law of the Lotus Sutra."

But many volumes have been written to plumb the depths of meaning locked up in this simple sounding mantra. That is partly due to the fact that the title given to every sutra is seen to be immensely important and is considered to embody the entire teaching that it contains. As Nichiren Daishonin explains by analogy with the name of Japan:

*"Included within the two characters representing Japan is all that is within the country's sixty six provinces: the people and animals, the rice paddies and the other fields, those of high and low status, the nobles and the commoners...similarly included within the title, or daimoku, of Nam-myoho-renge-kyo is the entire sutra consisting of all eight volumes, twenty eight chapters, and 69,384 characters without the omission of a single character...the title is to the Sutra as eyes are to the Buddha."**

Moreover, Chinese is an incomparably concise language in which each character can be used to express an immense range of different though related meanings, so that these five characters combine to convey a universe of thoughts. But neither of those partial explanations can begin to convey the depth of meaning that Nichiren himself ascribes to this phrase. He describes it as the Universal Law of Life that expresses the relationship between human life and the entire universe. It sums up within itself he says, nothing less than the *"wisdom of all the Buddhas.*

Shakyamuni expresses something close to that in The Lotus Sutra itself, when he says that this Law, *"can only be understood and shared between Buddhas."*

That is not in any way referring to some sort of exclusivity. Far from it since the whole purpose of the Lotus Sutra is to convey far and wide the central concept of the universality of Buddhahood? It is simply saying that words and explanations can only take you so far along the path, you have to practice Buddhism, and experience to some extent its power and potential in your life, before you truly begin to understand it.

You have to bite into the strawberry before you can begin to understand what it tastes like. So I don't think we should be surprised or taken aback, if we find some of these issues elusive and difficult to grasp when we first encounter this practice. Buddhism is daily life and since life is infinitely complex, Buddhism inevitably will reflect that complexity.

In my own case I have to say I did find it difficult. It was one thing coming to understand the principles that underlie Buddhism, and appreciating just how valuable they could be close to, in terms of human relationships, and further afield perhaps, in terms of how society functions. It was quite another to commit to the practice of chanting a strange mantra, perhaps an hour or more a day. Did I really want to do that? A mantra moreover that carries with it a whole bundle of meanings and associations and implications that are to some extent closed off from everyday experience, derived from a quite different culture. That was quite a struggle. I started chanting, for two principle reasons. The people I met who were practising were to be admired in many ways, positive, compassionate, socially responsible, always constructive in their aims and objectives. But above all it seemed to me that there was only *one* way of coming to understand the true value of Nichiren Buddhism in my daily life, and that was to *allow* it into my life.

You don't have to understand *theoretically* what this phrase means when you begin chanting, in order to gain the benefits that it will bring. The understanding will come as your practice grows. You certainly don't have to hang on to the many layers of meaning locked up in its characters as you chant. It is not an intellectual process in that way. Nor indeed, in my experience, is it a *feeling* one, in the sense that you should expect an emotional response. You chant Nam-myoho-renge-kyo in a steady rhythm, as loudly or as quietly as you choose, or as your environment allows, freeing the mind off from any particular concerns, relaxed, listening to the rhythm of the voice, feeling the vibration in the body. The key thing perhaps above all, is to enjoy the moment for what it is. If you are thinking about what other more valuable things you could be doing with your time, then it's probably better that you go off and do them.

But that having been said, Buddhism clearly teaches that anything resembling blind faith, is not an acceptable basis for practice. Does it work? Is it making any difference? Nichiren argues consistently that it is up to us to pose these questions to ourselves. Take nothing on trust, however interesting, however powerful and profound the teaching. Unless it actually enables us to do something better with our lives; overcome problems, feel a greater sense of confidence in our own abilities, a greater sense of well being, become more focused on what we are seeking, then what is it for?

As we have seen, in Buddhism the word "faith" is related not to some external force, but to the strength of our belief in ourselves, in our inner resources of courage and wisdom and compassion, and our ability to harness them in our daily lives. We may indeed take up the practice initially because we come to value some quality that we see in the Buddhists we meet, or because we are attracted by what they say about the promise embodied in the practice. But in the long run, we can only continue our practice with commitment when we are aware of benefits emerging in our own life. That is certainly true of my own experience. I began slowly, and it was a real struggle for a time, a real struggle. But as I became aware of this profound sense of well being that ran right through my life, I started getting up an hour earlier each morning, wherever I was, at home or on location, so that I could do 45 minutes or so of chanting to launch me into the day.

Before we move on, let me attempt a fractionally more detailed and yet wholly practical account of the meaning of Nam-myoho-renge-kyo. Not one that carries us off into the deeper realms of Buddhist philosophy perhaps, in case we get lost without trace in such a vast territory, but one that might serve as a working reference, bearing in mind that if it stimulates you to know more you can seek out one of the references in the bibliography.

Nam.

So, the word *Nam* comes from the Sanskrit word *namas* and although it is commonly translated as, *to devote oneself to*, it has a very wide range of meanings. Perhaps the most important among those are the phrases *"to summon up,"* or *"to awaken,"* or *"to draw forth,"* or *"to make great effort."* Why is knowing about these different meanings helpful? Because they express subtle differences in our approach or our state of mind when we are chanting at different times. When we are faced with something of a crisis for example we may well be thinking about summoning up, or making great effort, rather than just awakening.

Myoho

Myoho describes the profound relationship between the very *essence* of life, or the life force inherent throughout the universe and the literally millions of physical forms in which that life force is manifest or expressed. In Buddhism, everything that is, sentient and insentient, is both a manifestation of that life force, and subject to the eternal rhythm of life that we have talked about, formation, continuation, decline and disintegration. Everything is subject to that process of change, of impermanence as it is often called.

As Nichiren Daishonin defines that thought,

*"Myo is the name given to the mystic nature of life, and ho to its manifestations."**

Myoho is made up of two elements, *myo*, which refers to the unseen or spiritual element that is inherent in all things, and *ho*, which refers to the tangible, physical manifestation that we can apprehend with our senses. In Buddhism all things, all phenomena have a *myo* aspect and a *ho* aspect. They are two different but inseparable aspects of life, "two but not two," as Buddhism expresses it, as inextricably interlinked as the two sides of a coin.

Thus the *ho* aspect of a painting for example, is made up of the canvas and the paint that is spread across it. The *myo* aspect is the feeling or the emotion or the creative energy within the artist as he applied the paint in a particular way, and the emotional impact upon us as we view it. Music similarly has a clearly recognisable *ho* aspect in the arrangement of the black and white strokes or the notes on the page, and the physical vibrations produced by the instruments as they interpret them. The profound *myo* aspect is the effect the music has on our emotions and feelings, as we receive the sounds produced by the instruments in that particular sequence. As Shakespeare expressed it so pithily in *Much Ado About Nothing*, it is wholly inexplicable that a sequence of sounds produced on violin strings made out of the gut of a sheep- can move our heart so readily to tears!

If we think of ourselves, *ho* is used to refer to all the elements in our physical make up that can be observed with the senses, our appearance, the way we stand, the way we walk and talk, the way we gesture with our hands and the various expressions we use to communicate. All the things in fact that enable someone to recognize us as who we are. But what is quite clear is that so many of those gestures and movements, the expression in our eyes and the tone and modulation of the voice, the animation in the face, the posture of the body are also an expression of our inner life, our *myo*. The two aspects are, as we have said, inextricably interwoven. As we practice and seek to strengthen the vitality of the *myo* or spiritual aspect of our lives, there is no question that it has a powerful effect upon our physical persona, the expression on our face, the look in our eyes, our tone of voice, our readiness to smile and so on.

Those are perhaps very obvious examples. Rather more difficult to accept, indeed one of the most difficult concepts to understand, particularly if you have a background in science I suspect, is the Buddhist belief that all material existence, everything on earth and in the universe, both animate and inanimate, has a physical and spiritual aspect. Everything but everything, we are told, has both *myo* and *ho*. The tree, the rock, the river, the mountain.

A difficult idea undoubtedly, although Buddhism of course, is by no means alone in holding this view. Throughout the length and breadth of human history, artists and poets have been constantly seeking to open our eyes to this truth, in all languages and in all cultures. Wordsworth for example, when he famously described the dance of a bunch of daffodils,

"The waves beside then danced; but they Outdid the sparkling waves in glee:
A poet could not be but gay,
In such a jocund company,
I gazed…and gazed…but little thought
What wealth the show to me had brought:
For oft when on my couch I lie,
In vacant or in pensive mood,
They flash upon my inward eye,
Which is the bliss of solitude,
And then my heart with pleasure fills,
And dances, with the daffodils."

Buddhism stresses this aspect of the continuity and association that runs through all things, so that we are not separate from, but closely linked to everything around us. Thus, in Buddhist terms, statements such as being in harmony with, or being at odds with one's environment are not simply casual figures of speech, they represent a fundamental truth; a truth that is the basis for the Buddhist principle of oneness of self and environment. This argues that as we change, gradually strengthening and revealing our Buddha nature through our practice, so that change resonates throughout our environment, sending out beneficial ripples in all directions.

One analogy that paints a graphic, if somewhat simplified picture of the relationship between our *myo* and *ho* is that of the horse and cart, or *horses* and cart to be more accurate. Our life is the cart, pulled along by our *myo* horse, or our deepest spiritual energy, and our *ho* horse, our physical life. In general its true to say that we are accustomed to spending a great deal of time and effort nurturing the strength and well being of our *ho* horse, because it is so visible and so physically accessible to us. We can look at it in the mirror for example, and worry about its shape. We can feed it three times a day, and take it to the gym to work out, and off to play sports to ensure that it's kept fit and healthy and suitably diverted. As a result we tend very much to equate our happiness or our sense of well being with how well we are getting on with looking after our *ho* horse.

By contrast we tend to spend relatively little time if any, nurturing and exercising our *myo* horse, because of course it is wholly unseen and in general has a less powerful presence. The result is imbalance. The wagon of our life is at best pulled strongly off in one direction, the direction governed by our physical needs. At worst it is pulled round and round in circles, repeating patterns of behaviour, because the spiritual side of our make up simply hasn't been nurtured enough to influence, to change that is, our habitual behaviour. We can become very much creatures of habit, tending to repeat patterns of behaviour even when they lead to pain and suffering. People very often for example go through a whole series of similar relationships, each one of which might follow a very similar pattern of rise and fall. What we need to do, Buddhism argues, is to become aware of the danger of imbalance, and to allocate more time and energy to keeping both the *ho* and the *myo* horses in a healthy state.

Renge

Renge means lotus flower. It also means cause and effect. The lotus flower, adopted as the title of Shakyamuni's ultimate teaching, is an immensely significant symbol in Buddhism for many reasons. It is a plant with a particularly beautiful flower that grows and flourishes most strongly, in mucky, muddy, swampy environments. In this sense it is taken to symbolise the great potential locked up in every human life, the promise that we can build strong and positive and flourishing lives, however difficult the circumstances and the environment we find ourselves in.

Moreover, the lotus happens to carry both blossoms and seed pods at the same time, simultaneously, and in this sense, it is seen to symbolize one of the fundamental and most important principles of Buddhism, known as the simultaneity of cause and effect. Once again it is a principle with which Buddhism asks us to challenge the way we are accustomed to thinking about our everyday lives and relationships. Basically it argues that every cause we make, good, bad and indifferent, plants a balancing effect in our lives, that will, without fail, sooner or later, make itself felt. Thus there is, for all of us, an on-going chain of causes and effects. That is, if you like, the fundamental dynamic of our lives, it ties together the past and the present and the future.

Buddhism argues that only by coming to understand this can we grasp fully what it means to take responsibility for our actions, and change those inherent tendencies that are causing us to suffer. So it is a fundamental teaching that has all sorts of ramifications, since we are, of course, making causes all the time, within our own lives and in relation to the lives of those with whom we come in contact, all day every day, in everything we do and say and think. Good causes, good effects; bad causes, bad effects.

That process of linked causes and effects is going on all the time. So, in other words, *where* we are now, *who* we are now, how we act now, could be seen as the sum of all the causes we have made in the past, that have planted effects in our lives.

At the same time, the causes we are making now contain the seeds of our future. So, that is saying, the key factor in shaping our lives is how we respond to the situations that face us now. However much we might feel it to be the case, we are not simply subject to chance and accident that come at us out of our environment. The key factor is how we respond to those situations, the causes that we make, and therefore the effects that we generate. The basic message of hope is that whatever has happened in the past, good positive causes made now, will plant good effects in the future.

Kyo

Just as with *myoho* and *renge, kyo* has many meanings, but it is literally translated as"sutra"or the voice or teaching of the Buddha. It also means, vibration, or sound. So it can be taken to represent the vibrations that spread out from someone in the process of chanting. Indeed there is a common Buddhist saying that *"the voice does the Buddha's work,"* and there is no question that the sound or the vibration that is created by a group of people chanting together, even quite a small group, can be very powerful indeed.

I can still recall with great clarity for example, the very first Buddhist meeting I went to, some time before I actually started practising. It was a dark, cold winter evening, I remember, and we were walking along this street of narrow Victorian houses in West London, with me thinking not particularly positive thoughts, such as *"Oh well, It can't last more than about an hour, this meeting"* And then as we turned up the short garden path to the house, coming through the closed front door there was this wonderful resonant sound. Strong, confident, vibrant. It actually made the hair tingle on the back of my neck I remember. A sound produced by just a dozen or so ordinary people, chanting Nam-myoho-renge-kyo.

This has been necessarily an all too brief account of the many meanings locked up within *Nam-myoho-renge-kyo*, meanings that go on being added to and deepened as one's practice goes on. As I've said, it is a continuous journey, a continuous process of discovery.

This practice, focused around the chanting of Nam-myoho-renge-kyo is Nichiren's great legacy to humankind. Nichiren was in many ways a modernist and he makes it clear in his writings that it was fashioned specifically for ordinary people, no matter what place or period they inhabit, 13th Century Japan or 21st century Europe. People with busy everyday lives and much else to grab their attention, to enable them to understand that in the very midst of life's difficulties, it is possible to build lives of unlimited hope and optimism and resilience, and yes, great happiness too.

Understanding The Gohonzon

The Gohonzon is a simple rice paper scroll and it marks out Nichiren Buddhism from all other forms of Buddhism. It is its distinguishing characteristic. Hinayana or Theravada Buddhism, is very much focused on Shakyamuni Buddha, and the worship of him as a unique human being. Mahayana Buddhism, by contrast is very much more concerned to bring Buddhist teachings into the daily lives of ordinary people everywhere, and in Nichiren Buddhism, the Gohonzon, allied to the chanting of the title of the Lotus Sutra, Nam myoho-renge-kyo, make up the primary means of achieving that aim. The word *'go'* in classical Japanese means "worthy of honour," and *'honzon'* means "object of fundamental respect," so it is clearly an object that is held in the very highest esteem in Nichiren Buddhism. It is also, I have to say, an object of considerable beauty.

The Dai Gohonzon, Dai means *"great"* or *"original,"* was inscribed by Nichiren on 12th October 1279. The original Gohonzon that he inscribed is still preserved in Japan, at a place not far from Tokyo, but anyone who is prepared to make the personal commitment to practice in accordance with the principles of Nichiren, and to protect and care for their own Gohonzon, receives a smaller block print version to enshrine in their own house. This is how members of the SGI practice. It is, I should emphasise, an entirely lay movement, there are no priests. Nichiren himself, during his lifetime, established this pattern of individuals receiving a personal Gohonzon, to make it easier for them to practice in a place of their own choosing.

Not long afterwards he wrote,

"I Nichiren have inscribed my life in sumi ink, so believe in the Gohonzon with your whole heart"*

Sumi is a form of ink used particularly in Japanese calligraphy, and with that immensely simple phrase Nichiren sums up the scale of the task that he had accomplished. He made it abundantly clear to his followers that he regarded it as nothing less than the fulfilment of his life- long mission as a teacher of men.

The characters on the scroll, in Chinese and Sanskrit script, are there to represent the entire reality of human life, and right down the centre, in bigger and bolder characters than the rest and, as it were, illuminating all of the human life they represent, are the characters, *Nam-myoho-renge-kyo Nichiren.*

That bold central inscription is the key to understanding the nature and the intent of the Gohonzon. When Nichiren wrote, *"I have inscribed my life in sumi."* he is talking about his life as a Buddha, or in the state of Buddhahood. So we have it there in front of us, a representation of what it is that we are seeking to draw out from within our own life, nothing less than our highest life state. It is his great gift if you like, to all of humanity, and in that sense it embodies the fundamental Buddhist principle, first declared in the Lotus Sutra, that all ordinary human beings have the potential for Buddhahood, inherent within their lives.

It is difficult to think of an accurate analogy that comes close to expressing what it is that is going on when you chant in front of the Gohonzon. One that comes close is perhaps the musical one. When Beethoven or Mozart for example sat down and wrote out a piece of music, they too were expressing their life state, their passion, their spirit, their elation or melancholy, at that moment in time. An inner world transmuted into bold marks in black ink on white paper. Whatever happens subsequently to that piece of paper, the spirit that flowed through the writer's inner world, at that time, has been indelibly inscribed on it, for all of time. The sheet of paper with the ink marks could rest unnoticed on a dusty library shelf for decades on end. It could be copied out lovingly by a clerk's hand, or put through a modern digital photocopier to churn out a thousand copies. But whatever journey it travels, when the thousandth copy is placed in front of a musician and played, the *spirit* embodied in the original all those years ago, is, to a greater or lesser extent, brought back to life to fill the room with its sound and its vibration, and to recreate in those who hear it, some measure of the spirit that went into it when it was written.

With the Gohonzon, we, in this analogy occupy the role of the musician. We are seeking to recreate the spirit embodied in the original. The Gohonzon depicts all the aspects of our ordinary human life, the good the bad and the ugly, the positive and the negative, the light and the dark. All these aspects of our everyday lives are there, and Nichiren's too, for he was after all an ordinary human being. But they are illuminated by the principle that can enable us, however strong our anger or however deep our despair, to move our lives towards the life state of Buddhahood, that Nichiren captured in sumi ink. Nothing is excluded. No life state is rejected. We don't have to get rid of anything, or feel guilty about anything. The structure of the Gohonzon is there to make clear, that there isn't a life state or a condition that a human being can experience that would in some way prohibit that journey towards our greater self. Everything can be transformed.

That is the huge scale of the promise.

And that really is the Gohonzon's basic purpose, it is something physical to focus on. It is that practical. Something to keep our mind on the task in hand, namely chanting. Nichiren has given us this *'picture'* of what it is we are seeking to achieve. It is nothing more than that. Nor, it is important to remember, nothing *less*.

It is sometimes described as a mirror, that reflects back to us our true nature. Just as we cannot see our face without a mirror to reflect it back to us, so Nichiren argues, we cannot perceive our Buddhahood without the 'mirror' of the Gohonzon to reflect its image.

Does it really happen? Yes. Undoubtedly, and for many thousands of people. Can we clearly say why? I do not believe so. There are many explanations offered but all too often the explanations are couched in terms that are no less mystical than the events in front of the Gohonzon. But then many things in our universe lie beyond the scope of the partial and incomplete vision provided by our intellect.

What the practice in front of the Gohonzon *does* require is real application and effort, and a commitment to persevere, to give it your best shot. Of course there are ups and downs. You stride forward one month and stand still the next. But the stark reality of course, is that people only continue with this practice because of the benefits that appear in their lives. That has to be the acid test, and the implications are profound. We are not talking about a heaven of whatever form in some hereafter, coming as a reward for the way one lives in this life. Buddhism, as we have said so often, is daily life. This life, in the here and now. The benefits have to be felt at home and in the workplace and in how one feels about life today and tomorrow and the day after.

There is no test more strenuous than real life.

Chapter Sixteen

A New Beginning

I started off on this long journey into Buddhism with no small measure of reluctance. I cannot say that there was at the start any clear vision or sense of direction. There wasn't an overriding idea or an obvious goal towards which I was heading. There was however, I now realize, an inner resolution. There seemed to be no point otherwise. If I try to put myself back in that situation, I was determined that once I had set out I would continue on the journey until I was sure, one way or the other, about the value of this practice in my daily life. It was easy enough for people to say to me "Buddhism *is* daily life," the question was, did it actually work at that level? Did it make a fundamental difference to the way I viewed the mundane stuff of every day?

In my reading and particularly in my conversations with people who practise, I had gained a glimpse that it might well do that. When I went to Buddhist meetings there was a genuine sense of optimism, even when people were talking about all kinds of difficulties and challenges. Life was about seeing the problems for what they were, challenging them, and converting them into opportunities for change. Ordinary people, with ordinary everyday problems, learning to see life differently, through the focusing lens of the practice.

The greatness of this practice in my view, is precisely that. It enables us to achieve that slight shift in perspective. And strange as it may seem, that is all that is needed. It may only be a slight change, but time and time again it proves to be enough to tackle the problem with a completely different attitude, that then leads on, to tangible, positive, sometimes even dramatic changes, in someone's life. And every time it does so, it strengthens the resolve to deal with the next issue that comes along in the same way. We move from being generally anxious and negative about problems, to being focused and positive about them.

But it goes well beyond simply coping with our life's difficulties, however large they may loom in our eyes at the time. It is important not to lose sight of a wider perspective.

What we have been discussing in this book has focused for the most part, on the way in which Buddhist practice can help us, as individuals to understand our lives, and to develop happy and productive relationships within a relatively close environment. The fact is of course that those are the relationships, which have by far the biggest influence on our lives. They make up the fabric of our lives from day to day and from week to week. Maintaining harmonious relationships even within this relatively narrow circle, takes enormous effort and energy.

But that having been said, perhaps the biggest challenge now facing all of us as individuals, is learning how to extend this understanding, this compassion that the practice helps us to develop, out beyond the circle of our friends and colleagues and work mates, out beyond our own society, out beyond our own country, out to embrace all of humankind. At first glance that may well sound like no more than wishful thinking. No

more than a thin pious hope. The history of man's inhuman-
ity to man is so devastating that it can drive out the hope that
such a change can ever be achieved.

There is however a growing body of opinion that seeking to
achieve it is the unique challenge of this generation. In the
BBC's annual series of Reith lectures for 2007 for example,
the noted American economist Jeffrey Sachs, launched his
thesis on the possibility of achieving such a global synthesis,
with the following sentiments;

*"I want to talk about the challenge of our generation. Ours is not
the generation that faced the challenge of Fascism. Ours is not the
generation to have first grappled with the nuclear demon,
although we still grapple with it today. Ours is not the generation
that faced the Cold War.......Our challenge, our generation's
unique challenge is learning to live peacefully and sustainably, in
an extraordinarily crowded world....*

*Most importantly for us on this crowded planet, facing the chal-
lenge of living side by side as never before, and facing a common
ecological challenge that has never been upon us in human
history until now, the way of solving problems requires one
fundamental change. A big one. And that is learning that the
challenges of our generation are not us versus them. They are not
us versus Islam. Us versus the terrorists. Us versus Iran. They are
us, all of us together on this planet, against a set of shared and
increasingly urgent problems."*

There is no doubt that we find it extraordinarily difficult to
extend understanding and compassion to strangers in any
sustained way. The pictures of natural disasters and man
made tragedies in different parts of the world, that more and
more frequently crowd our television screens, may undoubt-

edly stir our compassion to the point of sending off a contribution to some charity. That we think, is just about the only
helpful gesture that we can make. But then the 24 hour news
machine grinds on relentlessly to the next drama, the next
crisis, and the old one fades rapidly into the background

Even with the very best intentions, it is incredibly difficult to
sustain compassion for other people much beyond our
immediate circle. One could well argue that that very inabil-
ity lies at the root of many, if not most of the major problems
confronting modern societies. To talk of a Global Village may
be a truism, but that doesn't make it any less true. We
certainly live in a world where nowhere is very far away any
more; where what happens in a lonely valley in Afghanistan
or in a dusty village street in Palestine or in a wayside café in
Indonesia, can have an intimate and devastating effect on
lives right across the world.

Socrates famously said that we instinctively seek what is
good for us. Most ordinary human beings want world peace.
Most ordinary human beings believe that to be an unattainable ideal, and in any case there doesn't seem to be any path
along which it can be achieved. Buddhism reminds us, *every
single day*, of two powerful truths. However difficult it may be
to achieve, it remains a desirable and meaningful goal.
However difficult the path, it starts right here, with each one
of us. We can begin moving along it whenever we choose. It
involves coming to understand with our whole life, that we
are not powerless, that through our individual actions we can
have a profound and beneficial effect upon our environment.

Daisaku Ikeda has made it his life's mission to spell out for
us the wider social and indeed global implications of this
practice. He writes

"In an age when both society and the religious world are wrought by turmoil and confusion, only a teaching that gives each individual the power to draw forth his or her Buddha nature can lead all people to happiness and transform the tenor of the times. In other words the only way to realize happiness and peace for people in the latter day is by developing our great human potential. There can be no substantial solution to the problems of society that does not involve developing our state of life."*

THE END

List of References

Page 9. Professor Arnold Toynbee. *Choose Life* (with Daisaku Ikeda)

Page 15. Nichiren Daishonin. *Writings of Nichiren Daishonin. (WND) Vol. 1.* p 1137

Page 19. Brian Greene. *Fabric of the Cosmos*

Page 23. Robin Dunbar. *New Scientist. February 2006.*

Page 25. Daniel Dennett. *Kinds of Minds.*

Page 62. Richard Causton. *Buddha in Daily Life.*

Page 73. WND Vol. 1. p 3.

Page 73. WND Vol.1 p 386.

Page 85. Daisaku Ikeda. *World of the Gosho. Vol. 1.*

Page 89. Martin Seligman. *Time Magazine. February 2005.*

Page 91. WND Vol. 1 p 601.

Page 97. WND Vol. 1. p 302.

Page 98. WND Vol. 1. p 302

Page 107. Professor Arnold Toynbee. *Choose Life (with Daisaku Ikeda).*

Page 123. Daisaku Ikeda. *Faith into Action.*

Page 144. Daisaku Ikeda. *Faith into Action.*

Page 150. Daisaku Ikeda. *Faith into Action.*

Page 159. Richard Feynman. *The Character of Physical Law.*

Page 159. WND Vol 1. p 3

Page 160. Professor Arnold Toynbee. *Choose life (with Daisaku Ikeda)*

Page 164. Jacob Bronowski. *The Ascent of Man.*

Page 165. Richard Feynman. *The Character of Physical Law.*

LIST OF REFERENCES

Page 167. WND Vol.1 p 932

Page 170. Daisaku Ikeda. *Notes to Painting a World of Friendship Exhibition*

Page 179. Michael Marmot. UCH London . *Study on Stress.*

Page 183. Professor Richard Layard. *Happiness.*

Page 183. Sonja Liubomirski. UCLA. *Time Magazine. Feb. 2005*

Page 197. Charles Atkins. *Modern Buddhist Healing.*

Page 201. Dr. Carol Shively. *The Journal of Biological Psychology. Nov. 2004.*

Page 222. WND Vol. 1. p 106

Page 223. Daisaku Ikeda. *World of the Gosho. Vol.1*

Page 248. WND Vol 1. p 386

Page 250. WND Vol 1. p 922

Page 254. WND Vol 1. p 4

Page 262. WND Vol 1. 412

Page 270. Daisaku Ikeda. *World of the Gosho. Vol 1.*

BIBLIOGRAPHY

Advice on Dying and Living a Better Life   His Holiness
   The Dalai Lama
First published: 2002 by Rider, an imprint of Ebury Press,
   Random House, 20 Vauxhall Bridge Road, London SW1V
   2SA.

Kinds of Minds   Daniel C Dennett
First published: 1996 by Weidenfeld & Nicholson. Paper-
   back edition published 1997 by Phoenix, Division of
   Orion Books Ltd, Orion House, 5 Upper St Martin's
   Lane, London WC2H 9EA

The Buddha in Your Mirror   Woody Hochswender, Greg Martin
   & Ted Morino
First published: 2001 by Middleway Press, a division of the
   SGI-USA, 606 Wiltshire Blvd, Santa Monica, CA 90401,
   USA.

The Character of Physical Law   Richard P Feynman
First published: 1965 by the British Broadcasting Corpora-
   tion. Published with a new Introduction in Penguin
   Books 1992, Penguin Books Ltd, 27 Wrights Lane,
   London W8 5TZ.

Buddhism A Short History   Edward Conze
Reissued 2000. Published by Oneworld Publications (Sales
   & Editorial), 185 Banbury Road, Oxford OX2 7AR.

Choose Life A Dialogue   *Arnold Toynbee and Daisaku Ikeda*
Published by Oxford University Press 1989, Walton Street,
   Oxford OX2 6DP.

Going Buddhist   *Peter J Conradi*
First published in 2004 by Short Books, 15 Highbury
   Terrace, London N5 1UP.

The Fabric of the Cosmos   *Brian Greene*
First published in the USA by Alfred A Knopf 2004.
   Published simultaneously in Great Britain by Allen Lane
   2004. Published in Penguin Books 2005, Penguin Books
   Ltd, 80 Strand, London WC2R 0RL.

The Buddha in Daily Life   *Richard Causton*
First published as **Nichiren Shoshu Buddhism** by Rider
   Books in 1988. Paperback edition published in 1995 by
   Rider, an imprint of Ebury Press, Random House, 20
   Vauxhall Bridge Road, London SW1V 2SA.

Mahayana Buddhism   *Paul Williamson*
First published in 1989 by Routledge, 11 New Fetter Lane,
   London EC4P 4EE; 29 West 35th Street, New York,
   NY 10001.

On Being Human   *Daisaku Ikeda, Rene Simard, Guy Bourgeault*
First published: 2003 by Midleway Press, a division of SGI-
   USA, 606 Wilshire Boulevard, Santa Monica, CA 90401,
   USA.

The Living Buddha   *Daisaku Ikeda*
This book originally appeared in Japanese under the title
   Watakushi no Shakuson-kan (My View of Shakyamuni),
   published by Bungei Shunju, Tokyo 1973.

First English edition, 1976. Published by Weatherhill, Inc,
568 Broadway, Suite 705, New York, NY 10012, USA.

The Power and Biology of Belief   *Herbert Benson*
New York, Scribner 1996.

Healing Words. The Power of Prayer and The Practice of Medicine
  Larry Dossey
Harper. San Francisco 1993.

Mind Body Medicine   *Daniel Goleman and Joel Gurin*
New York. Yonkers 1993.

Emotion. The Science of Sentiment   *Dylan Evan*
Oxford Paperbacks 2002.

The Progress Paradox   *Gregg Easterbrook*
Random House Trade 2004.

Authentic Happiness   *Martin Seligman*
Free Press 2003.

The Wisdom of the Lotus Sutra   *Daisaku Ikeda*
World Tribune Press 2000.

Makiguchi: The Value Creator   *Dayle M Bethel*
Weatherhill Inc, New York 1973.

The World of Nichiren Daishonin's Writings: Vol 1   *Daisaku Ikeda*
Sokka Gakkai Malaysia 2003.

*Lectures on the "Expedient Means" And "Life Span"
  Chapters of the Lotus Sutra*   *Daisaku Ikeda*
World Tribune Press 1996.

BIBLIOGRAPHY

Conversations & Lectures on the Lotus Sutra: Vol 1   *Daisaku Ikeda*
SGI-UK 1995.

Conversations & Lectures on the Lotus Sutra: Vol 2   *Daisaku Ikeda*
SGI-UK 1996.

Happiness   *Richard Layard*
First published in the USA by The Penguin Press, a member
    of Penguin Group (USA) Inc, 2005.

INDEX